Academic Literacies Provision for International Students

Lia Blaj-Ward

Academic Literacies Provision for International Students

Evaluating Impact and Quality

Lia Blaj-Ward
Nottingham Trent University
Nottingham, UK

ISBN 978-3-031-11502-8   ISBN 978-3-031-11503-5   (eBook)
https://doi.org/10.1007/978-3-031-11503-5

This Palgrave Macmillan imprint is published by the registered company Springer Nature
Switzerland AG.
The registered company address is: Gewerbestrasse 11, 6330 Cham, Switzerland

A THANK-YOU NOTE

For a number of years now, the academic literacies provision I design and deliver to students enrolled on various degree courses at a UK university has been closely mapped onto the learning outcomes of those courses and has helped students build their knowledge and confidence to engage in their academic journeys to the best of their ability. The students who attend my group sessions and individual tutorials start their courses with varied levels of language proficiency and prior experience of academic study through the medium of English. The distance they travel will inevitably differ from student to student, but individual student success is in no small part due to the collaborative set-up of the provision, with academic, subject specialist colleagues opening up their practice for scrutiny and helping unpack their expectations with regard to standards of academic work on the courses they lead and/or teach. Over the years, I have learnt that furthest distance travelled or best outcomes are always secured as a result of designing academic literacies provision for students, with students and with colleagues. I have also become aware of the importance of encouraging the more proficient language users in each setting to make more salient, for the benefit of their less confident peers, the language necessary to articulate ideas in ways that do full justice to the complex thinking that students put into their academic work. Although I am the only named author of this volume about quality and impact, the insights I am sharing have been arrived at as a result of years of reflective scholarship- and research-informed dialogue with students and a wide range of colleagues, to whom I am extremely grateful.

A special note of thanks goes to Conrad Heyns, Yvonne Cavanagh and all colleague assessors on the BALEAP course accreditation scheme for being part of my learning journey about impact and quality of academic literacies provision.

The vignettes in the volume—Kay (Chaps. 1, 3 and 5), Lucy (Chap. 3), Amber (Chap. 3) and Constellations University (Chaps. 2, 4 and 5)—are a composite of features of many different learning experiences I have had over the years. There is no intended direct resemblance to specific individuals or settings. The example of "A designer's guide to colouring-in a literature review" in Chap. 3 is modelled on a project with substantial input from Christopher Hanley.

KEYWORDS

Academic literacies; Quality assurance; Quality enhancement; International student experience

CONTENTS

1 **Introduction**   1
  Remembering...   1
  A Brief Note on the Broader Policy and Strategy Environment   3
  Academic Literacies Provision   5
  Quality and Impact   7
  Wellbeing and Sustainability   11
  *A Brief Note on My Professional Learning About Quality and
  Impact*   12
  Chapter-by-Chapter Overview   16
  References   18

2 **Institutional and Sector Perspectives on Impact and
  Quality of Academic Literacies Provision**   21
  "The Impact Cannot be Measured with Precision, But..."   21
  *Understanding the Institutional Context and Parameters of
  Academic Literacies Provision*   23
  Data on Quality and Impact: The Institutional Perspective   26
  Measuring Impact: Language Gain and Learning Gain   30
  *Assuring Quality: External Examining and External
  Accreditation Processes*   35
  *A Note on Making Quality and Impact Part and Parcel of the
  Natural Rhythm of an Institution*   38
  References   40

3   Experiencing Impact and Quality: International Student Journeys   43
Opening Section   43
Exploring International Student Experiences of Academic Literacies Provision at University   44
Scenario 1 of 3: Student-Led Evaluation of Assignment-Focused Academic Literacies Provision   49
Scenario 2 of 3: Impact Beyond Course Completion   53
Scenario 3 of 3: Co-creating Academic Literacies Provision with Students   58
Closing Section   61
References   63

4   Creating Impact and Quality: The Role of Academic Literacies Practitioners   67
An Opening Note on Wellbeing   67
Care-full, Impact-full Pedagogies for High-Quality Learning   70
Practitioners as a Source of Impact and Practitioners as Evaluators   73
Practitioner Approaches to Academic Literacies Scholarship   79
A Closing Note   85
References   86

5   Conclusion   89
Rethinking Boundaries in Academic Literacies Provision and Evaluation   89
Pandemic-Related Challenges and Opportunities for Quality Evaluation and Enhancement   93
References   96

Index   99

CHAPTER 1

Introduction

REMEMBERING…

Late afternoon, early May 2020, Kay arranges her coloured pencils tidily back in their box. She is two-thirds of the year into a postgraduate Graphic Design course, a speaker of English as an additional language in an English-speaking country. Her first language does not have a specific word for wellbeing, but Kay has been trying to capture the concept in her drawing, not least because temporarily the boundaries of the world she lives in have narrowed substantially and her wellbeing has been impacted by a phenomenon she only recently learnt the word for: a pandemic. The lively university campus that was meant to be the backdrop for Kay's year-long journey of academic and personal growth is almost completely deserted. Teaching has moved out of lecture theatres and seminar rooms and studios and is now streamed into the student accommodation space. Kay's studio flat is light and airy, and her relatively comfortable personal circumstances mean that she can focus her attention on her creative work. She travels virtually to galleries and museums across the world. Her summer travel plans across a continent are now paused. Walking to the local supermarket is the longest journey she has been able to make over the past month or so.

Within Kay's immediate peer network, some students have travelled back to their home country to be in what their families perceived as a safer environment. The scheduling of synchronous online learning experiences is now dependent on the range of time zones to which the students have dispersed. Outside Kay's immediate peer network, however, student experiences of cross-border academic mobility are impacted by a wider range of factors and to a larger and, in some cases, more negative degree. Narratives of relative privilege sit alongside narratives of uncertain subsistence.

L. Blaj-Ward, *Academic Literacies Provision for International Students*, https://doi.org/10.1007/978-3-031-11503-5_1

1

> *Behind the scenes, Kay's university is working hard to ensure that Kay's and her peers' learning experience is disrupted as little as possible; that academic and personal growth are facilitated in ways that lead to maximum positive impact for individuals and the communities and localities to which they belong; that it learns from the experiences of Kay, her peers, and those of staff and other stakeholders, and creates new, sustainable ways of working that benefit all who study, work or are connected in some form or another with Kay's university.*

The present volume focuses on one particular aspect of international students' experience at university—academic literacies provision, aimed at building students up as competent, confident communicators in a variety of contexts related to their university course. The label "international" is used throughout the volume as shorthand for speakers of English as an additional language (EAL), pursuing degree-level study through the medium of English in a context where English may or may not be the language spoken beyond the university campus gates. It includes speakers of English as an additional language who may be classed as "home" or "local" for fee-paying purposes in the context in which provision is delivered.

In Spring 2020, contexts, practices and pedagogies associated with academic literacies provision underwent substantial transformation. The virtual contexts, redefined practices and richer pedagogies are gradually making their way into the core of the profession. In the absence of an appropriate point for comparison, to ensure the continued relevance and impact of what we do, as academic literacies professionals we now more than ever before need to ask ourselves questions about the best evidence basis on which to make decisions and ways to arrive at those decisions. The present volume considers a range of answers to these questions. It explores conceptual nuances of quality and impact with regard to academic literacies provision. It looks at tools to gather quality and impact data. It takes account of various rationales behind choice of processes and procedures to generate relevant evidence that can effectively underpin decision-making in a transformed higher education (HE) context. It does not prescribe solutions; it offers options for providers to consider and adapt given the particularities and specific nature of each institutional context.

A Brief Note on the Broader Policy
and Strategy Environment

In the UK, the context from which I derive my professional experience, pandemic-related changes to international student higher education experiences are being made against a supportive national policy backdrop. The UK government's 2019 *International Education Strategy* (HM Government 2019) and the updated 2021 version (DfE and DfIT 2021) offer a strong basis on which recovery and growth from the pandemic can be effectively planned. The updated 2021 document reiterates the belief in the UK higher education sector's "world-leading reputation for quality" (p. 4) and in the need to "develop impactful and innovative activity to support [international] students to succeed" (p. 27). Strategy aspects of particular relevance to the present volume are as follows:

- The streamlining of immigration processes and in particular of the graduate route, which signals the UK's commitment to welcoming international students and to supporting their aspirations beyond graduation
- Increased attention to creating a coherent journey for international students from application to graduation and employment and access to career building opportunities
- Emphasis on collaboration across official bodies, sector agencies and higher education institutions (e.g. Universities UK International, British Universities' International Liaison Association, the Association of Graduate Careers Advisory Services, the UK Council for International Student Affairs, the Office for Students and the British Council working in partnership to generate evidence, build networks and make recommendations with regard to international student experiences of UK higher education)
- Recognition of the increased role of transnational education (TNE) and a commitment to reframing the narrative about the quality of TNE provision

These aspects are filtering down through redesigned internationalisation and global engagement strategies within each higher education institution (Lewis 2021). They inform the setting of priorities within various areas of each institution and the concerted actions taken to redesign higher education experiences for international students joining courses on campus or online.

Higher education provision is gradually changing in response to macro-level strategic steer. International students' participation in higher education is also changing, bringing about the need to reshape and realign academic literacies provision and to gather quality data to inform this process. As framed in Action 5 in the UK Government's *International Education Strategy* (DfE and DfIT 2021), it is essential to explore "'what works' in ensuring international students can integrate and receive a fulfilling academic experience" (p. 28) and to capture insights from the response to the pandemic which will have longer-term relevance and usefulness. While some of the new developments and insights will be specific to the UK context, it is highly likely that a substantial proportion will resonate with provision through the medium of English in a variety of national higher education systems across the globe where English may or may not be the official language of communication outside the university campus gates.

With regard to data about "what works", the executive summary of an OECD (2020) report highlights the following:

> Many national governments are working on initiatives to improve the data available to assess the performance of higher education. These initiatives cover areas as diverse as the standardised assessment of student outcomes, implementing large-scale surveys of student satisfaction and collecting more granular labour market outcome information on graduates. International efforts to develop new methodologies and standards for the collection of data on higher education outcomes and policies also represent important steps forward in the development of the evidence base to measure higher education performance.

Macro-level initiatives at sectoral, national and international level, as described in the OECD report or exemplified in the UK-based initiative by the Quality Assurance Agency around transnational education, are mirrored by initiatives within individual higher education institutions to capture rich and relevant evidence to evaluate and enhance educational experiences. Data about the quality and impact of academic literacies provision, designed to facilitate learning journeys on degree-level courses, is often difficult, if not impossible, to disaggregate from the core surveys that higher education institutions are required to implement. Local, complementary processes need to be designed to facilitate the implementation of individual institutions' strategic ambitions (Lewis 2021) in ways that lead to academic and personal growth for students like Kay in the opening vignette, as well as other international students with a variety of prior learning experiences and future-oriented aspirations. The present volume offers evidence and reflective commentary to support the development of such processes, with a specific focus on academic literacies provision.

ACADEMIC LITERACIES PROVISION

For the purposes of this volume, academic literacies provision refers to a specific category of learning and teaching activities organised by providers of higher education through the medium of English. These activities are designed to facilitate a fuller academic experience for international students for whom English is not the first language. They help increase awareness of key aspects of communication relevant in academic contexts and, at the same time, develop their English language proficiency. To design academic literacies provision effectively, various strands of research and scholarship need to be drawn on: applied linguistics, language learning and higher education pedagogy. To fully achieve its purpose, provision needs to be informed by research and scholarship generated both externally and locally to the institution, in the specific context where it is delivered. It also needs to be aligned to relevant policies and strategies (at macro, meso and micro level). A commitment to fine-tuning provision, on an ongoing basis, in response to particular needs and aspirations of each new cohort of international students joining an institution is also a fundamental requirement.

"Academic literacies" is a concept with a complex history. It was originally used in the seminal 1998 article by Lea and Street, to refer to a specific approach that responded more closely to student needs in the context of widening student participation in UK higher education. It was contrasted to study skills (perceived as generic and assuming unproblematic transfer across different academic contexts) and academic socialisation (perceived as imposing a set of norms and expectations, rather than allowing students to grow their academic identity in a way that did not erase or devalue their prior experiences and their learning from across a range of life experiences). It focused primarily on ways to use language and to construct meaning and identity in academic settings. In its initial stages it did not intersect with academic and practitioner debates about language development for international students. The original concept has informed many pedagogic initiatives across a variety of disciplines and contexts, discussed in a substantial body of literature. Lea (2016) revisits discussion about the concept, the field and its theoretical allegiances and underpinnings from the perspective of one of the lead authors associated with academic literacies. Hilsdon et al. (2019) offer an external viewpoint on the evolution of academic literacies through a crowd-sourced synthesis of insights. A selection of additional sources are referenced throughout this volume.

The use of the phrase "academic literacies" in the plural in this volume is designed to reflect a broader focus than a core academic discourse which assumes an audience with a particular type of specialised, theoretical knowledge. It does so in order to do justice to learning experiences that integrate activities outside the classroom doors or campus walls. English for Academic Purposes (EAP), the area most immediately recognised as supporting international students' academic success, was in its early stages focused on distilling and teaching the specialised features of academic discourse as used by bounded academic communities. Originally, EAP professional debates and practice took place in a different space to that in which academic literacies work unfolded (e.g. Lillis and Tuck 2016). The connection between EAP and academic literacy/ies has developed over the years, with EAP gradually encompassing a broader range of pedagogic scenarios. A quick look at relevant publishers' catalogues and journal table of contents will show how EAP scholarship and research have grown and diversified in recent years.

While mindful of the risk this poses, the present volume uses the label "academic literacies" as a placeholder for a broad range of provision. "Academic" should be interpreted as referring broadly to the higher education context (given that university curricula now integrate more fully learning experiences which previously fell into an extracurricular category and which respond to a renewed focus on supporting students' aspirations beyond graduation). "Literacies" carries with it an acknowledgement of plurality and of the importance of attending to specific contexts in which provision is developed and delivered. The pandemic-induced online pivot added another layer of complexity to communication in university contexts, with digital technology foregrounding some aspects which previously played a less central role. The use of "academic literacies" throughout the volume is inclusive of the literacy components identified by Roche (2017) and Ahmed and Roche (2021), namely, socio-cultural, language, critical, institutional and digital, with each provider being invited to consider carefully the way in which these are most effectively balanced and integrated for the benefit of students.

The volume focuses on academic literacies in English. An extensive body of literature on English-medium education in multilingual university settings has developed in recent years. A key focus for discussion is the scope for students to draw on multilingual repertoires in the process of developing as "resourceful speakers" (Pennycook 2019) or language users. Dafouz and Gray (2022, p. 169) pose a number of highly pertinent questions in relation to bi- and pluri-literacies:

> For instance, how does the multilingual and translanguaging stance advocated here align with the linguistic constraints within which institutions, countries, and their citizens [...] have to operate? What are the language requirements graduates may face on seeking employment? What, we might ask, would a lingua franca English look like in professional settings, and how might it be developed? And, in this vein, how does this lingua franca align with the growing understanding that biliteracies and pluriliteracies are needed so that twenty-first-century citizens and professionals can operate both locally and globally?

The present volume acknowledges the importance of these questions; however, a focus on the choice of language (in addition to English) lies outside the scope of this volume. Instead, discussion centres on literacies—on core academic literacies and on how the core is enriched (as opposed to diluted) if some degree of attention is given to relevant literacies from outside a narrowly defined academic remit.

QUALITY AND IMPACT

In the higher education context, quality carries multiple meanings. It is experienced, assured and evaluated differently by different stakeholders. Pechmann and Haase (2022) note that it is "an inherently ambiguous research topic and a multitude of concepts and terminology have been proposed to capture it" (p. 355); an extensively cited article by Harvey and Green (1993) identifies five facets of quality, three of which resonate particularly well with ongoing debates about academic literacies provision: fitness for purpose (as defined by the provider or by those who experience education), value for money (accountability to organisations or individuals who fund the education) and transformation, linked to enhancement or empowerment. The present volume looks at aspects of quality from the viewpoint of institutions, students and practitioners. Each chapter explores one of these viewpoints in turn. Chapter 2 focuses on the institution perspective and takes a macro view of quality both as a form of external accountability, with implications for the profile and reputation of an institution, and as an array of policies and processes which ensure adequate institution-wide management of quality. Chapter 3 puts the student perspective at the centre of the volume, exploring student perceptions of quality on a micro, individual level, and student engagement in quality-related processes. Chapter 4 takes the perspective of academic literacies practitioners; it focuses on approaches that academic literacies practitioners have adopted to evaluate the quality and impact of provision at course and module level.

At an institutional level, quality is associated with an external regulatory requirement applicable across the higher education sector. In the UK, the context from which the author derives her professional experience, higher education institutions are bodies with degree-awarding power and set their own academic standards in alignment with a series of external reference documents. This activity was underpinned, at the time of writing the volume, by the Quality Code (QAA 2018), a document which "articulates the fundamental principles that should apply to higher education quality across the UK" (p. 3) and acts as a reference point for higher education providers with regard to delivering a high-quality education experience that meets and exceeds sector-recognised standards. The use of external expertise is fundamental to meeting regulatory requirements, and it is how the sector helps maintain the credibility of its degrees. External examiners of degree courses provide impartial and independent scrutiny of student achievement in relation to standards. They input into the design, development and approval stage of a course. They are given access to sufficient and timely evidence and invited to highlight delivery and monitoring aspects that could potentially impact on standards.

Within the remit of quality assurance, care is taken that effective processes and procedures to evaluate and enhance provision are adhered to. Depending on where the providers are in the quality journey, these processes and procedures may be at different stages of development. To ensure that they fully support quality, it is essential that processes and procedures evolve and are fine-tuned in ways that fit the natural rhythm of an institution. It is also essential that an action plan is included, as a living document, guiding quality enhancement activity, supporting the development of a shared understanding of aspects that can be improved and coordinating a response to them.

Academic literacies provision may be credit-bearing, in which case formal quality assurance processes and procedures in use within any one institution may apply. However, this is not necessarily the case. Given the wide variety of forms that academic literacies provision can take and the presence or absence of direct assessment of learning in the context of the provision, its quality may be assured and enhanced in a variety of context-specific and context-sensitive ways and its impact may be experienced and captured through a variety of methods. With regard to high stakes provision which has a bearing on student readiness to enrol on a university course, Roche and Booth (2021) offer an insightful discussion of standards and quality assurance approached collaboratively, cross-institutionally in the Australian context.

In the context of the present volume, the impact of academic literacies provision refers primarily to the learning that students derive from experiencing the provision and their perceptions of how they have benefitted from this. This learning may be evidenced through grades received, but grades are only part of the picture. The learning may be closely mapped onto the intended learning outcomes (Biggs and Tang 2011) stated in the course documentation or it may be incidental, tangential or serendipitously connected to planned activities but of equal value to students. A complementary understanding of impact is from the perspective of staff—evaluating provision can lead to staff development within an organisation, to provision enhancement and to disseminating insights externally for the benefit of other professionals in the wider sector.

The volume is premised on the assumption that the academic literacies teams involved in designing provision agree learning outcomes, consider ways of establishing to what extent the planned outcomes have been achieved (which may or may not include formal summative assessment of learning), and select and sequence activities to scaffold the students' learning experiences towards the point where outcomes are achieved satisfactorily. Design choices are informed by an understanding of the degree-level course which academic literacies provision precedes or is interwoven with. They are also informed by an understanding of the kinds of prior knowledge and educational experiences students bring with them and of the expectations they have with regard to the academic literacies offer and their aspirations for life beyond university.

The volume is also premised on the assumption that as academic literacies provision goes through several iterations, it is continuously enhanced. To support enhancement fully and effectively, quality assurance processes which are internal to an institution need to be built seamlessly into the provision. They need to respond to the rhythm of an institution and to give parity of consideration to all stakeholder views.

Where learning is evaluated via a pass/fail system or specific grades, a high-quality course aims for pass rates as close to 100% as possible after a range of circumstances have been factored in. It supports students to achieve at the highest level possible in alignment with their own goals and given their pattern of engagement in the course. It offers learning experiences that facilitate maximum engagement. It sparks curiosity and a desire to learn more. It develops effective learning approaches in the students.

At the stage of designing provision, the team will want to articulate the basis for their design choices to ensure these are appropriately sound and evidence-informed. The notes can be used to frame criteria against which the provision is continuously evaluated. All stakeholders should input into the development of the evaluation criteria, although in different institutions different expectations about which stakeholder group defines quality (and who makes the final decision on ways in which quality is measured) will apply. In the case of high-quality provision, quality assurance processes permeate the provision rather than being an add-on. There are mechanisms for students to feed back on an ongoing basis and mechanisms to close the feedback loop. Stakeholders have realistic expectations about the nature of changes that can be implemented in response to their views. They are encouraged to engage with the process in a personally meaningful way.

Quality and impact are created and confirmed with reference to an evaluation strategy, which may exist as a formal written document or as tacit knowledge among the academic literacies team. A strategy underpins processes and procedures which respond to set purposes. The processes and procedures reflect whose viewpoint matters in a given context, who is most likely to benefit from the evaluation outcomes, how stakeholders are engaged and how collaborative the evaluation experience is designed to be. Insights from an evaluation may be used internally or may be disseminated externally via published outputs. If open to a broader audience, the insights need to be fully contextualised to maximise their useability and relatedability. Evaluation processes have substantial resource implications and may run the risk of not being implemented in a way that generates sufficiently deep and meaningful information.

WELLBEING AND SUSTAINABILITY

A conversation about evaluating the quality and impact of academic litera-cies provision cannot sidestep explicit references to wellbeing and sustain-ability. In "normal" as well as in pandemic-shaped circumstances, learning and learner wellbeing are inextricably linked. The pandemic has placed a spotlight on wellbeing. Examples of recent studies which draw out wellbe-ing implications of academic experiences include Huang et al. (2020), who focus specifically on international students in Australia, and Colaiacomo (2020), who unpacks the concept of wellbeing in the context of curriculum internationalisation in the UK. The pandemic has drawn attention to the resource required by student services colleagues to reach out to international students in culturally sensitive ways. It has also drawn attention to the need to intensify the support available and empathise more fully with challenges experienced by international students when the journeys they had undertaken across continents and deep waters to learn, grow and develop turned into distressful experiences of not being able to return home to loved ones. It has also, very importantly, drawn attention to the need to make wellbeing a core consideration when developing and designing academic curricula—and implicitly academic literacies ses-sions—rather than it being viewed as a separate strand of university experi-ences. Various contributors to *Narratives of Innovation and Resilience* (Blaj-Ward et al. 2021) share stories of innovation and resilience in aca-demic literacies in which wellbeing figures repeatedly. A recent UNESCO (2021) report on the future of education emphasises the importance of achieving wellbeing through participatory collaboration, rather than as an individual activity. Emerge Education and Jisc (2021) offer foresight for universities and start-ups on how wellbeing can be achieved at scale.

Alongside wellbeing, sustainability is and should continue to be a core focus in the pandemic-transformed higher education landscape. Carefully rethinking the education offer available to international students will ensure that physical mobility options strike the right balance between environmental sustainability and creating maximum learning value for stu-dents. At the same time, the accelerated inclusion of sustainability as core content across curricula and disciplines and as a defining feature of life on physical or virtual campuses (UNESCO 2021) will increase the engage-ment with sustainability as carrier content for academic literacies develop-ment sessions. Lastly, sustainability should permeate the processes of designing and evaluating academic literacies provision. This provision is most likely to achieve its aim when it is fully aligned with the university course experience that students are ultimately aiming to undergo. University learning overall has been transformed by a global pandemic with an uneven geographic distribution. However, in the run-up to the pandemic (as well as a result of this) it had begun to change in recognition that society needs university curricula that are a better fit for the future, responding to the fourth industrial revolution and other opportunities and challenges along the way (Coonan and Pratt-Adams 2018). Change is likely to be ongoing and at a faster pace than before. Agile realignment of academic literacies provision is required, and there are opportunities and challenges to achieve this in a sustainable way.

A Brief Note on My Professional Learning About Quality and Impact

My journey of learning about quality and impact is underpinned by a keen interest in exploring the most appropriate array of data to make decisions about educational provision. It is also underpinned by a commitment to integrating evaluation into the students' learning experiences as part and parcel of the pedagogic processes. To reflect on my learning, I have captured this in writing. A number of publications I have authored or co-authored are listed in chronological order, for the benefit of colleagues within the sector and, implicitly, that of the students whose academic success they support. Laying my perspective open for scrutiny is intended to help colleagues who work in contexts very different from mine to borrow and adapt principles in ways that best align to their education systems and environments and to feed back on their experience to support others' development.

The present volume is preceded by two other Palgrave publications: *Researching Contexts, Practices and Pedagogies in English for Academic Purposes* (2014) and *Language Learning and Use in English-Medium Higher Education* (2017a). The reading and reflecting I engaged in during the process of writing these two books helped develop and consolidate my professional knowledge about quality assurance and enhancement processes. In the 2014 volume, I dedicated a separate chapter to discussion about quality, relevance and impact of academic literacies provision. Saunders et al.'s (2011) edited volume was a particularly salient source which guided my learning about evaluating educational provision in higher education—the view they put forward of evaluation as social practice informed my choice of material to include in that chapter. Two contributions in particular, Shreeve (2011) and Shreeve and Blythman (2011), both discussing alternative approaches to evaluation which were sensitively attuned to ways of learning in specific subject areas, stood out for me.

Saunders et al. (2011) also sensitised me to the potential lack of congruence in how stakeholders perceive—and therefore assure and evaluate—quality in teaching and learning. This insight led me to Sovič (2013), a study which foregrounds the value of international student perspectives. Sovič drew on interviews conducted in the students' own language by their peers to highlight commonalities and differences in perceptions of good-quality academic experiences. Methodologically, it presented a valuable alternative to a typical end-of-module questionnaire, the standard format through which student perceptions of teaching and learning are sought in higher education. I used Sovič's study as an example to emphasize the importance of fine-tuning the process of capturing views and perceptions and ensure that all stakeholders contribute equitably to decisions designed to enhance teaching and learning, a view of quality I fully subscribe to.

At the time of writing the 2014 volume, I was in the early stages of my involvement with the BALEAP course accreditation scheme, a quality assurance and enhancement framework originally set up to focus on courses which prepared international students for study at a UK university (BAS: BALEAP's course accreditation scheme). Recently revised (BALEAP 2022), BAS is a multifaceted scheme which explores the way provision is delivered within an institution, contextualises it within the institution's broader learning and internationalisation strategies, and benchmarks it against good practice in the sector, making suggestions and recommendations related to enhancement areas and approaches. To inform their evaluative comments, recommendations and enhancement guidance, BAS assessors (of which I am one) carry out document analysis, observe live or pre-recorded learning and teaching events, and gather insights through meetings with stakeholders in the institution whose provision they are invited to accredit. My experience of BAS informed a number of questions I asked in my 2014 volume—included below—which I have continued to explore in my professional practice and scholarship:

- Where the quality assurance process involves a reviewer who is external to the provision being assured, what level of subject expertise is the reviewer required to have?
- In the case of quality assurance taking place in house, how are roles and responsibilities for different aspects of provision distributed across the academic and professional services team members?
- In order to achieve the goal of being developmental, how are quality assurance processes integrated with quality enhancement processes?
- Do all stakeholders have a clear sense of ownership of the quality assurance process and does this translate into practice?
- What standards can be used to evaluate provision against?
- What criteria can be used to evaluate the provision?
- What counts as evidence that quality, standards and information are adequately managed and maintained?
- What arrangements should be put in place to adequately capture the student voice for quality assurance and enhancement purposes?
- At what stage in the quality journey does the provision find itself? (Blaj-Ward 2014, pp. 149–150)

The 2014 volume mapped key academic and professional debates relevant for English for Academic Purposes provision from the viewpoint of practitioners planning to conduct or commission research into learning, teaching, professional development or quality assurance in EAP. My second Palgrave volume, *Language Learning and Use in English-Medium Higher Education* (2017a), is a counterpart to that. In Blaj-Ward (2017a), I explored international students' experience of English for Academic Purposes from their viewpoint, contextualising insights from interviews within relevant literature. The second volume was prompted partly by a desire to build a basis from which to challenge the assumption that language development at university is an inevitable consequence of exposure to language both in and out of formal instruction contexts. Quality and impact are the focus of Chap. 6 ("Parameters of English language development provision in EMI")—particularly with regard to tracking, a methodology that several studies have attempted to use in order to establish the value of EAP/academic literacies provision for students. Tracking assumes an increase in ability to communicate in academic environments and relies on language tests among other tools. The literature review I carried out when writing Blaj-Ward (2017a) confirmed that commercially available tests measure only general proficiency, and that objective/formal instruments for assessing language gain in EMI contexts are notoriously difficult to design, given that they need to capture individual development, with different starting and end points and interim milestones. The student interviews I conducted in preparation for that volume were an opportunity to explore the academic and informal networks that impacted on international students' competence and confidence as language users. I reflected on using those insights for quality enhancement purposes, to inform provision design. I also reflected on the balance between encouraging international students to proactively join informal networks in a variety of contexts and setting up formally facilitated ones. I noted that access to social relationships in situations where students are perceived as valued partners in communication (as opposed to being positioned as a deficient language user in an unequal power relationship) were more likely to lead to positive outcomes in the case of my interview participants. I made the case that all stakeholders should be sensitised to the importance of language development brokering (see also Blaj-Ward 2017b) in supporting users of English as an additional language in English-medium higher education contexts.

The experience my interviewees had of learning language for academic purposes was not limited to completing academic assignments; it involved complex identity work, and it connected to their career aspirations. I reflected on this further in a more recent piece of research (Blaj-Ward and Matic 2020) which invited students to choose one assessment which in their view had the most relevance for their career aspirations and explore the source of support they accessed to complete that piece of work. Within the UK policy landscape, documents developed shortly before the start of the pandemic gave employability increased salience and made it important to consider more fully how this can become a feature of academic literacies provision, not least because employability content is gradually being mainstreamed in the university curricula to which academic literacies provision is aligned, opening up opportunities to generate a more complex type of impact, more relevant and more meaningfully aligned to students' learning goals.

Another source of learning and professional development for me were my experience as external examiner for Coventry University's MA in Academic Writing Development and Research (2017–2020) and an Advance HE online course for external examiners which I took in 2020 (see reflective account in Blaj-Ward 2020). These experiences added depth to my understanding of formal institutional processes of quality assurance outside the immediate context of academic literacies provision.

Over the past ten years or so, the BALEAP course accreditation scheme has been a constant source of knowledge and insight for me. At the time of writing the present volume, the BAS scheme has just launched its revised accreditation criteria (BALEAP 2022), fine-tuned to respond to the diversification of academic literacies provision and to broaden the scope of the scheme beyond the UK context in which it originated. The disruption to higher education caused by the pandemic has led to changes in learning and teaching which are inevitably linked to impact evaluation and ways in which the quality of academic literacies provision is gauged. The redeveloped criteria were a logical next step in the developmental journey of the accreditation scheme and are framed and worded in a way that allows full and sensitive engagement with academic literacies provision that the pandemic has directly and indirectly reshaped.

CHAPTER-BY-CHAPTER OVERVIEW

Chapter 2 explores impact and quality in academic literacies provision from an institutional viewpoint. It frames evaluation as social practice and as an integral part of learning and teaching experiences. It unpacks key contextual parameters to be taken into account when carrying out a comprehensive, institution-wide evaluation of provision. It considers the type of data that can effectively underpin conversations about quality and impact. Discussion of attempts to measure language proficiency gain or learning gain is also included here, with reflection on methodological challenges. Emphasis throughout the chapter is on finding a context-specific appropriate balance between effort expended on measurement and evaluation and the perceived benefits of the enhancements put in place as a result. As partnerships between higher education institutions globally intensify to facilitate life-relevant collaborative learning opportunities (e.g. British Council 2021), developing a mature quality culture within a higher education institution is crucial to delivering high-quality, impact-full learning.

Chapter 3 places student lived experiences at the centre of discussion. It offers three scenarios for consideration: a student invited to evaluate academic literacies provision focused on a specific assessed piece of work; an opportunity to integrate evaluation of academic literacies provision with employability learning, linked to students' aspirations regarding careers and life more broadly beyond graduation; and a resource co-creation project with a wellbeing strand. Reflective, exploratory questions that can help tease out impact accompany each vignette. The chapter makes connections between needs analysis, unplanned, serendipitous learning opportunities, the transition from language learner to language user, language development brokers, assessment for employability learning, authentic assessment and student expectations of how academic literacies provision in a pandemic-shaped higher education context scaffolds their development as competent communicators and (digital) citizens. The ultimate aim of academic literacies provision is to enable students to communicate with confidence, clarity and care. Co-creation of learning experiences and resources is central to achieving this aim.

Chapter 4 adopts a practitioner viewpoint. It opens with a note on wellbeing and positive design as a reminder of the potential of academic literacies provision to support overall personal and professional growth and development for life beyond the campus walls. The chapter draws on Motta and Bennett's (2018) discussion of care-full practice and pedagogies of care to problematise quality assurance which leads to an instrumental higher education audit culture focused on measurable outcomes and transactional approaches. Three published studies from Australia, the UK and China, respectively, are included as illustrative examples of how generating and evaluating impact can be integrated in a variety of settings. To support impact evaluation, a five-level framework used in the context of staff learning and development is adapted specifically for student learning of academic literacies. The chapter discusses how generating scholarship helps practitioners explore and understand their practice with a view to enhancing its impact, as well as how collaborative scholarship can contribute to staff development.

Chapter 5 brings the volume to a close in two stages. The student experience relayed at the beginning of the volume is woven into a different vignette from my 2014 *Researching Contexts, Practices and Pedagogies in English for Academic Purposes*—to illustrate how the field and my understanding of it have developed. Priorities that began to take shape in the run-up to 2020 with regard to facilitating rewarding learning experiences in higher education acquired sharper contours as a result of the pandemic. The role of students and alumni in co-creating learning experiences, a key priority for higher education going forward, is highlighted through the merged vignettes. The second half of the chapter considers a number of pandemic-related challenges to quality and impact in academic literacies provision. It revisits the definition of academic literacies and puts forward evaluation principles to guide the way in which the multiple literacies that international students bring with them or familiarise themselves with at university can be integrated to support academic, professional and personal growth.

REFERENCES

Ahmed, S.T., & T. Roche (2021) Making the connection: Examining the relationship between undergraduate students' digital literacy and academic success in an English medium instruction (EMI) university. *Education and Information Technologies*, 26(4): 4601–4620. 10.1007/s10639-021-10443-0

BALEAP (2022) *BALEAP accreditation scheme (BAS) handbook*. BALEAP https://www.baleap.org/wp-content/uploads/2022/03/BAS-Accreditation-Hbook-v9x.pdf

Biggs, J.B., & C.S.K. Tang (2011) *Teaching for quality learning at university* (4th ed.). Open University Press.

Blaj-Ward, L. (2014) *Researching contexts, practices and pedagogies in English for Academic Purposes*. Palgrave Macmillan.

Blaj-Ward, L. (2017a) *Language learning and use in English-medium higher education*. Palgrave Macmillan.

Blaj-Ward, L. (2017b) From language learner to language user in English-medium higher education: Language development brokers outside the language classroom. *Journal of Research in International Education*, 16(1): 55–64. https://doi.org/10.1177/1475240917694109

Blaj-Ward, L. (2020) *Making external examining fit for the future*. Advance HE https://www.advance-he.ac.uk/news-and-views/making-external-examining-fit-future

Blaj-Ward, L., K. Hultgren, R. Arnold, & B. Reichard (2021) *Narratives of innovation and resilience: Supporting student learning experiences in challenging times*. BALEAP https://www.baleap.org/wp-content/uploads/2021/02/BALEAP-Narratives-of-innovation-and-resilience.pdf

Blaj-Ward, L., & J. Matic (2020) Navigating assessed coursework to build and validate professional identities: the experiences of fifteen international students in the UK. *Assessment & Evaluation in Higher Education*, 46(2): 326–337. https://doi.org/10.1080/02602938.2020.1774505

British Council (2021) *Role of international higher education partnerships in contributing to the sustainable development goals*. British Council https://www.britishcouncil.org/sites/default/files/role_of_international_higher_education_partnerships_in_contributing_to_the_sustainable_development_goals.pdf

Colaiacomo, S. (2020) Is everything OK? Internationalisation of the curriculum and constructions of wellbeing. In S. Turner & K. Kalawsky (Eds.). *Wellbeing in higher education* (pp. 11–14). SEDA Special 45.

Coonan, E., & S. Pratt-Adams (2018) *Building higher education curricula fit for the future.* Advance HE https://www.advance-he.ac.uk/sites/default/files/2019-05/Building-HE-Curricula-Fit-For-The-Future.pdf

Dafouz, E., & J. Gray (2022) Rethinking the roles of ELT in English-medium education in multilingual university settings: An introduction. *ELT Journal,* 76(2): 163–171. https://doi.org/10.1093/elt/ccab096

DfE & DfIT (2021) *International Education Strategy: 2021 update. Supporting recovery, driving growth.* DfE & DfIT https://assets.publishing.service.gov.uk/government/uploads/system/uploads/attachment_data/file/958990/International-Education-Strategy-_2021-Update.pdf

Emerge Education & Jisc (2021) *Student and staff wellbeing. Report 6.* https://repository.jisc.ac.uk/8276/1/student-and-staff-wellbeing-report.pdf

Harvey, L., & D. Green (1993) Defining quality. *Assessment & Evaluation in Higher Education,* 18(1): 9–34.

Hilsdon, J., C. Malone, & A. Syska (2019) Academic literacies twenty years on: A community-sourced literature review. *Journal of Learning Development in Higher Education,* 15. https://doi.org/10.47408/jldhe.v0i15.567

HM Government (2019) *International education Strategy global potential, global growth.* HM Government https://assets.publishing.service.gov.uk/government/uploads/system/uploads/attachment_data/file/799349/International_Education_Strategy_Accessible.pdf

Huang, L., M.L. Kern, & L.G. Oades (2020) Strengthening university student wellbeing: Language and perceptions of Chinese international students. *International Journal of Environmental Research and Public Health,* https://doi.org/10.3390/ijerph17155538

Lea, M.R. (2016) Academic literacies: Looking back in order to look forward. *Critical Studies in Teaching and Learning,* 4(2): 88–101. https://doi.org/10.14426/cristal.v4i2.91

Lea, M.R., & B.V. Street (1998) Student writing in higher education: An academic literacies approach. *Studies in Higher Education,* 23(2): 157–172. 10.1080/03075079812331380364

Lewis, V. (2021) *UK universities' global engagement strategies: Time for a rethink?* Vicky Lewis Consulting https://www.vickylewisconsulting.co.uk/global-strategies-report.php

Lillis, T., & J. Tuck (2016) Academic Literacies: a critical lens on writing and reading in the academy. In K. Hyland & P. Shaw (Eds.). *The Routledge handbook of English for Academic Purposes* (pp. 30–43). Routledge.

Motta, S.C., & A. Bennett (2018) Pedagogies of care, care-full epistemological practice and 'other' caring subjectivities in enabling education. *Teaching in Higher Education*, 23(5): 631–646. 10.1080/13562517.2018.1465911

OECD (2020) *Benchmarking higher education system performance.* OECD https://www.oecd-ilibrary.org/sites/e9434bba-en/index.html?itemId=/content/component/e9434bba-en

Pechmann, P., & S. Haase (2022) How policy makers employ the term quality in higher education policymaking. *Scandinavian Journal of Educational Research*, 66(2): 355–366. https://doi.org/10.1080/00313831.2020.1869081

Pennycook, A. (2019) From translanguaging to translingual activism. In D. Macedo (Ed.). *Decolonizing foreign language education: The misteaching of English and other colonial languages* (pp. 169–85). Routledge.

QAA (2018) *UK quality code for higher education.* QAA https://www.qaa.ac.uk/quality-code

Roche, T.B. (2017) Assessing the role of digital literacy in English for Academic Purposes university pathway programs. *Journal of Academic Language and Learning*, 11(1): A71–A87. https://journal.aall.org.au/index.php/jall/article/view/439

Roche, T., & S. Booth (2021) A collaborative approach to assuring standards: Using the CEFR to benchmark university pathway programs' English language outcomes. *Language Teaching Research Quarterly*, 26: 18–38. 10.32038/ltrq.2021.26.02

Saunders, M., P. Trowler, & V. Bamber (Eds.). (2011) *Reconceptualising evaluation in higher education: The practice turn.* Open University Press.

Shreeve, A. (2011) 'Tell us about it!' Evaluating what helps students from diverse backgrounds to succeed at the University of the Arts London. In M. Saunders, P. Trowler & V. Bamber (Eds.). *Reconceptualising evaluation in higher education: The practice turn* (pp. 181–185). Open University Press.

Shreeve, A., & M. Blythman (2011) Evaluating a UK Centre for Excellence in Teaching and Learning: Bottom-up evaluation in a top-down setting. In M. Saunders, P. Trowler & V. Bamber (Eds.). *Reconceptualising evaluation in higher education: The practice turn* (pp. 177–180). Open University Press.

Sovič, S. (2013) Classroom encounters: International students' perceptions of tutors in the creative arts. In S. Sovič & M. Blythman (Eds.). *International students negotiating higher education* (pp. 87–103). Routledge.

UNESCO (2021) *Reimagining our futures together: A new social contract for education.* UNESCO https://unesdoc.unesco.org/ark:/48223/pf0000379707

Institutional and Sector Perspectives on Impact and Quality of Academic Literacies Provision

"The Impact Cannot be Measured with Precision, But…"

The impact [of academic literacies provision] cannot be measured with precision, but it is likely to be influenced by the strategies that the management team uses to foster a culture of quality assurance and enhancement, by creating opportunities for staff to engage actively in the process in a personally meaningful way and by aligning the process with the natural operational rhythm of the institution. (Blaj-Ward 2017a, p. 155)

Academic literacies provision can be quantified in terms of hours delivered, staff costs or student numbers attending sessions, but its impact on student learning and achievement is far more difficult to measure and cannot be isolated from the very broad array of factors that contribute to student success at university. Given the complexity of learning experiences, any attempt to pin down a straightforward causal relationship will inevitably fail. Any attempt at quantitative measurement needs to be complemented with qualitative evaluations and carefully interpreted in context in order to generate a robust basis on which to make decisions about deploying resource and making changes. For measurements and evaluations to underpin the most appropriate decisions about resourcing and enhancing learning and teaching in higher education, they need to be woven into the fabric of the provision.

L. Blaj-Ward, *Academic Literacies Provision for International Students*, https://doi.org/10.1007/978-3-031-11503-5_2

The present volume is underpinned by the assumption that the impact which academic literacies provision aims to generate is international students' academic, professional and personal growth. The extent of growth will vary from individual to individual and will be influenced by a multiplicity of intersecting factors. Patterns will, however, emerge within and across courses; these patterns may vary over time. An array of evaluative practices is required to arrive at a nuanced picture of impact.

In the chapter which opens Saunders et al. (2011), Saunders (2011) defines evaluative practices as "sets or clusters of behaviours forming ways of 'thinking and doing' associated with undertaking evaluative activity, this includes the rooted identities and patterns of behaviour that characterise shape and constrain understanding of evaluative practice" (p. 2). Understandings of evaluative practices shape the way these are implemented. Clusters or constellations of practices are "cross-cut by horizontal and vertical considerations associated with distributions of power and resources, gender, ethnicity, identity/biography and place" (p. 3). Evaluative practices pervade higher education. Some are viewed as more legitimate than others (e.g. large-scale surveys and end-of-module feedback questionnaires), they are institutionally sanctioned and resourced, and the insights they yield underpin conversations within teams and departments about longer-term planning and enhancements to be put in place. Others are carried out on a day-to-day basis by individual practitioners and other stakeholders, focus on finer details filtered through personal experiences and viewpoints and may lead to immediate action. Both have a useful role to play in higher education in relation to academic literacies provision.

To start the conversation about measurement and evaluation as an integral part of learning and teaching experiences, the present chapter offers insights from sector-wide quality-related debates and frameworks that guide institutions' policies and decision-making with regard to academic literacies provision for international students. These act as a useful point of reference for designing, implementing, evaluating and enhancing provision. Providers engage with the debates and frameworks both as a form of external accountability and as an opportunity to develop an internal culture of quality.

Understanding the Institutional Context and Parameters of Academic Literacies Provision

In line with Saunders et al.'s (2011) view of evaluation as social practice, the first step when building a meaningful evaluative commentary is to develop an in-depth understanding of the nature of the provision whose quality and impact are being evaluated. To do so, it is important to be aware of the key parameters of the context in which it is delivered.

The provider's national higher education policy landscape, sector priorities, regulatory frameworks and any possible dependencies on higher education institutions located elsewhere in the case of transnational education (TNE) provision will influence the degree of visibility and the resource allocated to evaluate and enhance the learning experiences of English as an additional language (EAL) user students. In the UK, the Quality Assurance Agency publishes country-specific reports on quality frameworks and processes (e.g. QAA 2021a, 2021b). A scholarly perspective on quality assurance usefully complements contextual policy knowledge. Examples of relevant scholarly material on quality include Rosa and Amaral (2014), who map quality debates in higher education globally. Although the quality landscape has evolved in the meantime, the insights they provide still have valuable comparative purchase. Another relevant source, Neubauer and Gomes (2017) focus on higher education in the Asia-Pacific region. A comprehensive account of quality assurance in a specific national higher education context to which TNE provision may be linked or where EMI provision may be set up (Vietnam) is available in Nguyen and Shah (2019). The complexities of assuring the quality of cross-border higher education are discussed in Rosa et al. (2016) among others, with Trifiro (2021) making a recent contribution to the discussion of how quality assurance procedures have the potential to impact negatively on institutions' ability to develop innovative, collaborative, cross-border learning communities.

Within an institution, academic literacies provision links into two complementary strategies—the internationalisation (or global engagement) strategy and the learning, teaching and assessment strategy. It also has a ripple effect across other strategic ambitions and priorities, achieving impact both within and outside the curriculum, on campus and in the broader community. For example, provision can support students to complete a theoretical, academic piece of work which may inform actions that students take in the longer term but in the shorter term the academic piece of work remains within the private, confidential space of academic assessment. Provision can also align to consultancy-type, "live brief" assessments where the client is an external organisation and recommendations made in the assessment could be immediately implemented by the client.

Whether provision reports into a senior executive role within professional services or sits within an academic portfolio with allocated time for scholarship will influence how relationships are built with other academic areas, how quality is assured, what impact is valued and how impact is evaluated. The structural location, within an institution, of the organisational unit responsible for academic literacies provision, is a crucial aspect to bear in mind when discussing quality and impact. Structural location (as an academic department or a central professional services unit) will influence decisions on the way provision is integrated into formal quality assurance mechanisms within the organisation and on the quality assurance processes it adopts. Availability and choice of data and metrics, ease of access to relevant information and capacity to process this in a meaningful way, which loops back into the provision for enhancement purposes, are also determined by structural location. Evaluation of quality and impact carry resource implications.

The stage in the academic journey when provision is delivered is another aspect to consider from the outset. Academic literacies provision is offered to students at two stages in their university journey: prior to the start of a university degree course or during a course. Prior to the start of a university degree course, academic literacies provision can be offered in a standalone format (pre-sessional) or integrated into a foundation or graduate diploma course. In these cases, it is formally assessed and has a gatekeeping function. During a university course, it can be made available alongside credit-bearing subject modules, to facilitate students' academic success. In-course (in-sessional) provision often carries no credits on its own, although this is not always the case. In terms of focus and scale, where pre-sessional provision might place emphasis on language proficiency and might serve 10% of an institution's international student cohort, in-sessional provision could be made available to the full cohort looking at broader aspects of success within an academic environment, to a subsection of that cohort identified. Financial status is another way to differentiate between the two stages: pre-sessional provision usually generates separate income for an institution, whereas in-sessional provision is funded through degree course fees and makes a claim on existing resource.

This could potentially have a bearing on the resource available to secure external evaluation.

The degree of alignment of academic literacies provision to disciplines and subjects varies across institutions. Alignment also impacts on how fully integrated the provision is into an institution's formal quality assurance processes and whether it is written into the institution's official quality handbook, articulated as a formal policy or captured in teaching and learning enhancement projects with a university-wide or a local school or department remit.

The national geographic location in which education is experienced by students plays an important role in shaping academic literacies provision. In the academic and professional literature, discussion of academic literacies most often focuses on the experience of speakers of English as an additional language relocating to an English-speaking country for the duration of a full undergraduate or postgraduate course. However, other forms of study are also available, subsumed under a transnational education umbrella. English as an additional language students could, for example, be based in their home country and enrolled in degree course delivered by an English-speaking institution face to face, virtually or in blended mode. The degree course could be the outcome of a franchise, validation, progression or articulation agreement; it could be a joint or dual degree course, which may or may not involve some aspect of physical geographic mobility either for students experiencing the provision or for staff who facilitate it (Mercado and Gibson 2013). The relationship between the institution that awards the degree and the institution which delivers the education experience (if the two are different) has a bearing on the set-up of academic literacies provision—and implicitly on the way its quality is formally assured.

Transnational education is not the only way in which EAL students can access higher education through the medium of English outside an English-speaking country. Academic literacies provision could be developed in the context of EMI programmes (i.e. higher education delivered through the medium of English by institutions in countries where English is not the official spoken language). Yet another form of academic literacies provision could be aligned to shorter-term study exchanges (credit-bearing or not), delivered face to face or virtually. Lighter-touch or, conversely, more creative evaluation options may be considered in this situation.

Students' prior learning experiences have an important bearing on how students engage with academic literacies provision and on the learning distance travelled as a result of their engagement. Student engagement and perceptions are the focus of Chap. 3. Equally important to consider in relation to the way provision is designed and delivered are the nature of teaching contracts for staff, workload allocation, professional development and career progression. Practitioner involvement in scholarship is discussed in more detail in Chap. 4 in this volume.

DATA ON QUALITY AND IMPACT: THE INSTITUTIONAL PERSPECTIVE

An illustration of how the institutional context and parameters of academic literacies provision impact on the availability and readiness of quality and impact data to analyse and use as the basis for enhancement activity is provided in the following vignette:

Constellations University is located in an English-speaking country. It does not have, within its senior executive team, a dedicated role with an internationalisation portfolio. Internationalisation (through international student recruitment and support, collaborative cross-border learning projects, internationalisation of the curriculum and international research partnerships) is a strategic priority for the university but one that is progressed in different ways by different areas within the institution. Approximately one-fifth of students enrolled at Constellations University speak English as an additional language. A quarter of these are accepted on successful completion of a pre-sessional course run by a central unit within the university. The remainder are either direct entry students who have already met the English language proficiency requirements set by the university (slightly above-average sector level) or students who are enrolled on an articulation programme with a partner university abroad. For the latter, academic literacies provision in the home country is organised by the partner university.

At Constellations University, pre-sessional provision is delivered during the summer only by staff on fixed-term contracts recruited by a central unit with professional services status. In-sessional provision is organised by each academic school separately, through staff employed by the university on permanent academic contracts. In-sessional provision is mainly non-credit-bearing and fully embedded within subject areas.

A recent initiative, sponsored by the teaching and learning portfolio holder within the senior university executive team, aims to gather evidence to develop a coherent portfolio of academic literacies provision across the university. The focus of the initiative is not to prompt structural changes but to facilitate good practice sharing and to develop stronger connections between pre-sessional and in-sessional provision. There is anecdotal evidence that pre-sessional students perform less well in some academic subjects than in others and that some students who are highly likely to benefit from in-sessional provision do not access this on a regular basis. There is also scope to look more closely at integrating and streamlining support for international students throughout their journey at Constellations University as well as continuing this relationship with international alumni.

An institution in the situation similar to the one described above might use the following types of information to underpin discussions about creating a coherent, integrated academic literacies offer and form a basis on which to build evaluation of provision:

- Number of students classed as international for fee-paying purposes (allowing more granular analysis by country of origin)
- Number of students who speak a first language other than English (allowing more granular analysis by language spoken)
- Proof of English language proficiency level
- Whether students were required to complete a preparatory English language course prior to starting their degree and whether that was completed immediately prior to the start of the degree programme
- Whether students are joining through an articulation arrangement
- Whether students have completed a previous degree through the medium of English.

Alongside this, student performance data might yield relevant insights, if, for example, in-sessional provision supports students progressing throughout their degree from one year of undergraduate study to another, or using shorter time frames (terms, semesters or other timespans between assessments) for shorter courses.

Clear expectations about the use of data on student performance collected within an institution are set out by Tertiary Education Quality and Standards Agency (TEQSA's) (2020) *Guidance Note: Monitoring and Analysis of Student Performance*. The *Note* makes direct reference to the higher education sector in Australia but has immediate relevance to all providers of higher education, through the medium of English, to speakers of English as an additional language. Data that TEQSA advises providers to consider includes student grades and grade distribution as well as cohort-level rates of progression, completion and attrition, graduate out-comes and student satisfaction. Each individual provider is encouraged by TEQSA to consider their circumstances and to develop context-appropri-ate policies and processes to gather, analyse data and act on insights. Providers with substantial cohorts will be in a position to conduct com-plex statistical analyses, whereas smaller providers will benefit from engag-ing closely with qualitative data to understand factors which impact on the academic success of their students. What is important, however, is that all providers make principled use of evidence to enrol students who "have no known limitations that would impede their progression or completion" (p. 4) and to offer appropriate support to students, post admission, to engage as fully as possible with the course offerings. The *Guidance Note* recognises that not all risk of unsatisfactory performance can be identified and mitigated against from the outset, but careful engagement with the evidence will reveal factors associated with that risk and will offer a strong comparative basis on which to develop relevant interventions.

Some of this evidence will be captured and readily available in the stu-dent records that institutions hold. The digital platforms that institutions use for data capture will support or hinder the flexibility of systems to "speak" to each other so that queries can generate swift responses based on accurate data. Staff familiarity with the platforms' and systems' func-tions will also have a bearing on the relevance of data reports generated, as will planning time put into deciding which queries yield most value in terms of making decisions about resourcing provision and how best to integrate information from various sources. Dedicated data professionals who can generate reports and visualisations as a well as a good level of data literacy among decision-makers are paramount. Data about student satis-faction with academic literacies provision will also count towards decision-making, adding another layer of complexity. All quantifiable information needs to be carefully contextualised in a narrative which accounts for the unique features of any given instance of provision.

Discussion so far in this section has focused on the institution's per-spective, on the data that higher education institution staff gather and use as part of their core business. In my second Palgrave volume (Blaj-Ward 2017a, p. 118), I emphasised that academic literacies provision needs to

1. articulate with participants' prior and future experiences of academic literacies development;

2. frame its value in relation to participants' overall academic experience and their readiness to (re)join a globalised professional community;
3. empower participants to capitalise on formal and informal resources available;
4. engage participants in the decision-making processes around institutional resource deployment;
5. be embedded in a culture of quality that favours contextual sensitivity (i.e. quality processes should fit the natural rhythm of the institution and take account of the stage each institution is at in terms of its quality assurance journey).

Access to relevant, timely and accurate data—in ways that comply with data regulation requirements and fair and ethical data collection and processing in any given context—will support institutions to achieve the above-mentioned five points. It will also support them to go beyond a narrow focus on academic performance and look more broadly at how academic literacies provision impacts on international students' academic, professional and personal growth.

Data that relate to a specific cohort of students experiencing the provision can be complemented by longitudinal data about prior cohorts and about student experiences beyond graduation, some of which can be used to inform higher-level, overall decisions about resource allocation while others may support specific choices of content to include in academic literacies provision, delivery format or type of activity. While some of the data may be within easy reach, other information may need to be collected specifically for this purpose. Institutions may or may not have capacity to gather this data.

In further response to above-mentioned point (1), that is, "articulate with participants' prior and future experiences of academic literacies development" (Blaj-Ward 2017a), for pre-sessional provision data could be collected about students' expectations with regard to the degree course they wish to join or, for in-sessional provision, their understanding of the various stages of the degree course and of what is required to achieve successful progression from one stage to another. To address point (2), that is, "frame its value in relation to participants' overall academic experience and their readiness to (re)join a globalised professional community", the data collected could focus on how academic learning ties in with relevant co-curricular and extracurricular experiences or with students' career aspirations. Point (3), "empower participants to capitalise on formal and informal resources available", invites exploring access to informal study support networks (see Blaj-Ward 2017b for a discussion of the range of literacy brokers). In point (4), that is, "engage participants in the decision-making processes around institutional resource deployment", the reference to "participants" include both staff designing, facilitating and supporting the programme and the students for whom the provision is designed. Alumni could also be invited to feed into provision design to maximise potential learning benefits. Co-creation of academic literacies provision with students, at higher language proficiency levels but not only, can increase the likelihood of provision meeting student needs and expectations more fully. Contextual sensitivity (point (5)) is achieved through explicit conversations about data collection processes—the purpose they serve, the alignment with institution-wide approaches, the most appropriate timing, the resource available to capture, store and process the data, and the training that might be needed to do so. These conversations should include students as equal partners and should unfold in ways that add to wellbeing as opposed to creating an additional burden for all involved (Rahnuma 2020; Zozimo 2020). High-quality provision relies on continuous enhancement underpinned by carefully interpreted data that are reliable and relevant. Processes to generate and analyse data and to implement data-driven enhancement action should not be out of balance with the perceived benefit of the enhancement created.

MEASURING IMPACT: LANGUAGE GAIN AND LEARNING GAIN

In a pre-pandemic world, before March 2020, institution-level conversations about the quality and impact of academic literacies provision for international students were informed primarily by studies on various aspects of the relationship between language proficiency or gain and student academic performance outcomes. This involved attempts to establish a relationship between language test scores and academic grades (to establish predictive validity). Another frequently used format has been to compare language level at the start and end of an academic study experience to establish proficiency gains. The majority of work was conducted in the Australian context; the studies highlighted here illustrate the approaches taken, rather than focusing on the conclusions drawn from the analysis.

Using a sample of slightly over 5000 students, Oliver et al. (2012) compared the impact of different entry routes on undergraduate academic success measured through GPA scores (i.e. completing a pre-university foundation course vs holding an International English Language Testing System (IELTS) score above the minimum requirement). A recent review of research focusing specifically on the effectiveness of pre-sessional provision in UK higher education is available in Pearson (2020), who notes the limited research base in this area, maps the full range of methodological approaches employed to evaluate linguistic gain and highlights the variety of formats that university preparatory courses take, which has a bearing on the extent of impact they are likely to achieve.

Humphreys et al. (2012) focused on proficiency gains by comparing IELTS scores at the beginning and end of a semester for students already enrolled on an academic degree course. Similar to Humphreys et al. (2012), Storch and Hill (2008) focused on a semester-long experience, but developed their own in-house test of listening, reading and writing skills and explored possible test scores interpretations with the help of qualitative date derived through participant interviews. In the interviews, they looked beyond formal instructed language development opportunities and explored other opportunities students had to develop their language abilities. Formally set-up language support focuses on academic discourse but the nature of linguistic interaction that facilitates a successful academic experience on the university campus and in related spaces beyond campus walls is much more complex. Storch and Hill aptly caution that measures that quantify language proficiency gain may not be subtle enough to capture experiences of learning that do not have statistical significance but that do have substantial personal significance for international students in terms of how they experienced a course.

Storch and Hill's (2008) caution is echoed by Murray (2016) in a volume which focuses on standards of English in higher education. Murray's work calls attention to the need to ensure that international students who start their course with minimum proficiency levels are supported to increase these and develop into competent and confident communicators. The linguistic repertoire required to function successfully in a university context is broader than academic discourse, and language development at university is not solely within the remit of English language specialists. Humphreys et al. (2012) aptly frame this as a "complex tapestry of multiple intersecting conceptualisations of proficiency and multiple underlying variables" (p. 36). Arkoudis (2014) puts forward a case for making language development "everyone's business" (p. 17) and cautions that making provision available as a non-compulsory model of formal language support is unlikely to encourage participation from those students most in need. Lack of engagement with formal language support is highlighted in various studies, with implications not only for student success but also for the quality of data available to enhance provision.

Studies of embedded academic literacies provision, on the other hand, highlight improved pass rates and greater student satisfaction. Embeddedness is favoured by Murray (2016). Evans and Morrison (2012, p. 36) concur that generic, un-embedded provision is unlikely to achieve expected results; however, they strike a cautious note with regard to discipline-specific courses as well, drawing on a study with first-year undergraduates in Hong Kong: "evidence suggests that a raft of regular discipline-specific courses would have scarcely scratched the surface of their manifold and evolving needs; and only the most munificent university management would be prepared to sanction such a programme." Evans and Morrison also highlight that some participants in their research mentioned inspiring teachers as having a greater impact on their satisfaction than content—a useful reminder of the need to gather rich evaluative data on the multiple underlying variables of impactful learning experiences.

Institutions set a minimum required level of language proficiency for enrolment; however, this is met and exceeded in different ways by different students. Students have different starting points: some will benefit from substantial attention to language, others mainly from guidance on strategies to approach academic study and to fully demonstrate, through the assessments they complete, achievement of learning outcomes on a course. Gauging the impact of academic literacies provision in relation to increased language proficiency tells only a partial story and is methodologically challenging. Institutions need to be aware of these challenges so that they can focus their efforts and resources on the most relevant evaluative activities. Using language test scores and performance outcomes data may be more likely to yield useful information about provision that is more self-contained, for example a preparatory course that informs decisions about whether students can progress onto an academic course. They are less likely to do so in the case of embedded, in-course provision where comparison is attempted across courses with varying cohort sizes and different intended learning outcomes.

A complementary perspective on measuring gain, carried out on a larger scale and which has met with substantial methodological challenges of its own, is that of looking at learning gain more broadly in higher education (not with specific reference to academic literacies). Learning gain, as Tight (2021) indicates in a volume with broad international coverage, has been a focus of attention for higher education staff, policymakers and sector analysts and commentators recently. Tight cautions against prioritising resource for evaluating learning gain over resource for educational activity and using the former as a means to "give employers, policy-makers, the media and the general public yet more statistics to pore over, organise into league tables and become confused by" (pp. 11–12). A scoping report by Hoareau McGrath et al. (2015) is a useful starting point for a discussion about learning gain, not related specifically to international student experiences but highly relevant for this. The authors define learning gain as "the difference between the skills, competencies, content knowledge and personal development at two points in time" (p. 1). Their report, commissioned by the Higher Education Funding Council for England (whose responsibilities were transferred to the Office for Students portfolio in 2018) in collaboration with a government department for business and the main body supporting the professional development of higher education staff (then HEA, currently part of Advance HE), reviews evidence to support the launch of a pilot study to measure learning gain for a variety of purposes. Purposes for which the methods and tools would be used are as follows: "to inform improvements to learning and teaching; provide information to prospective students and their advisers; investigate the impact of particular learning and teaching interventions and contextual factors; assist in international comparison; or form part of the quality assurance of learning and teaching" (p. 4). The methods and tools Hoareau McGrath et al. (2015) highlight cut across the various purposes, and what is of particular relevance to the present volume is the critical perspective the authors offer on the suitability of these methods and tools to provide robust and comparable data across a wide range of institutions with different missions. With regard to mission, the authors note that "while learning gain is important, it constitutes only one aspect of several key missions of higher education, including, for example, research productivity, innovation and improving the capacity and diversity of the workforce for the labour market" (p. 12). The distinction Hoareau McGrath et al. (2015) make has acquired new meanings in light of the changes prompted by a global pandemic. Now more than ever, it is important to explore the interconnections between these several missions and look to capture the value of learning in terms of both individual development measured through grades and self-reported, evidence-based impact that individual learning has had on a wider range of stakeholders.

Hoareau McGrath et al.'s (2015) suggestion to "develop a new assessment of learning gain, based on academic collaboration around key disciplines" (p. 44) merits particular attention and should be extended to include all higher education areas that facilitate student learning, not just academic disciplines. While identifying discipline clusters around which collaboration should be built is not without its challenges, the benefits the authors identify are substantial enough to warrant putting effort into this endeavour: ownership of the process, transparency of information, collaborative benchmarking and building capacity among higher education communities to develop new methods and tools to capture learning distance travelled as part of studying at university.

To create a strong basis on which to build learning gain methodology that finds its appropriate place in the spectrum of purposes, from enhancement of learning and teaching to constructive, collaborative benchmarking, Hoareau McGrath et al. (2015) note that it is vital to start by articulating clearly the purpose of the methodology and explore ways in which this might lead to unintended consequences (e.g. gaming the system). Next comes deciding on level of disclosure of information (full or partial disclosure, to all or certain categories of stakeholders), on ownership by higher education institutions, the government or a sector body, or a commercial organisation, and on levels of accountability (national, institutional or other). The authors also flag up accountability and exchange of practice (data sharing), data protection (transparent procedures, consent and national legislation) and sustainability (the cost of the methods and tools, material or other forms of support, the official endorsement within the institution, and the sustained use of the method over time, to ensure initial spend is justified). These are important points to raise also with regard to academic literacies provision, in contexts where the provision may be delivered by a for-profit commercial organisation which has specific agreements with public higher education institutions.

The learning gain project discussed by Hoareau McGrath et al. (2015) was completed four years later, and an external evaluator report is available (Kandiko Howson 2019). Not surprisingly, as Kandiko Howson and Buckley (2020) note, the project failed to lead to the desired outcome: a sector-wide, institution-level measure of learning gain. Nevertheless, the search yielded useful insights to inform conversations about value and quality of higher education.

The challenges with measuring gain highlighted in this section with regard to either language gain or learning gain more broadly will hopefully serve as useful reminders to providers of academic literacies courses that the choice of evaluation approaches should be a critically informed one and it should be fully aligned with the delivery of the provision in order to yield genuinely relevant information.

ASSURING QUALITY: EXTERNAL EXAMINING AND EXTERNAL ACCREDITATION PROCESSES

The label "academic literacies provision" is used throughout the volume to signal the interconnectedness of language development and learning gain. The extent to which the interconnectedness is explicitly articulated, understood and enacted within an institution varies. To assure the quality of learning opportunities and some degree of parity across the sector, institution-external perspective is generally sought in higher education.

In the UK context, some academic literacies provision which is formally assessed is quality assured through external examining, a form of peer review which aligns to the way in which quality is assured on higher education courses which lead to a degree being awarded. Another option to receive external confirmation of the quality of academic literacies provision is to apply for BALEAP course accreditation (BALEAP 2022).

External examining is central to the successful functioning of the higher education system in the UK (Advance HE 2019). External examiners are usually appointed for a period of four years to review course learning outcomes, course specifications, assessment briefs, criteria and assessment outcomes, as well as course reports. They ensure that grading of student work is conducted rigorously and consistently. They provide specialist guidance in preparation for or during course validation and revalidation events. They complete reports in which they comment on the extent to which students who pass the assessments demonstrate they have achieved the intended learning outcomes, the overall performance of students and the pass rates. The reports also include commentary on the way student learning is assessed and on innovative features that the course could consider in relation to assessment tasks; on whether the assessment process is rigorous, involves equitable treatment of students, and is fairly conducted within regulation and guidance; and on the quality and quantity of feedback that students receive on assessed work. There is scope to consider potential risks and mitigations in relation to the broader learning experience. The examining process is also subject to scrutiny: examiners are invited to comment on whether the course team has engaged with their comments in a satisfactory way leading to improvements for the course and whether assessment boards are run according to regulations. In the UK, professional development for external examiners is provided by Advance HE (no date; see also Blaj-Ward 2020, for a reflective account of my learning experience on that course and Advance HE, 2019, for a more detailed overview of the external examiner system in the UK).

Over the four-year duration of their appointment, external examiners build a relationship with a course and witness its growth and development through the performance of several consecutive cohorts of students. They also act as critical friends, though their primary focus is on standards and processes. Examiners are advised to continuously update their knowledge of assessment scholarship so that, in turn, they can advise course teams about assessment design that best supports students to evidence how they have met course learning outcomes.

Another option for academic literacies provision to receive external validation of its quality is to apply for accreditation or endorsement, e.g. through NEAS (https://neas.org.au/quality-assurance/endorsement/) in Australia or BALEAP (https://www.baleap.org/accreditation/institutions). BAS (the BALEAP course accreditation scheme) is a scheme with voluntary participation for higher education institutions. BALEAP, the parent organisation of BAS, was set up in 1972 in the UK with the primary aim to "support the professional development of those involved in learning, teaching, scholarship and research in English for Academic Purposes (EAP)" (https://www.baleap.org/about-baleap/about-us). The course accreditation scheme was set up in 1991 and is open to institutions worldwide. Institutions which apply for accreditation have institutional membership of BALEAP and access to the events and resources the organisation makes available. Successful accreditation is awarded for a four-year period.

At the time of writing this volume, the BALEAP course accreditation scheme has just launched revised criteria aimed at evaluating provision on the basis of three core principles (contextualisation, constructive alignment and collaboration). These principles run through a set of 20 criteria, equally divided into two sections: (I) Administration and leadership and (II) Programme: content, delivery and assessment. BAS accreditation is awarded on the basis of document analysis and a visit carried out by assessors, who meet with a variety of stakeholders in the provider's institution (these consist of the team involved in designing, managing and delivering the provision; students; and senior management within the organisation).

The provider receives a report which offers comments about the effectiveness of evidenced practice against each criterion. Areas in need of attention are flagged up, recommendations are made and excellent practice is also signposted. The provider who puts a course forward for accreditation is required to submit accreditation context documentation, which offers a brief historical narrative of the organisational unit which houses the provision and information about priorities, collaborations, influence and impact. The provider is also required to specify the principles which underpin their provision and opportunities for professional development and scholarly activity they make available to staff in their context. A full set of additional documentation is listed in an appendix in the Accreditation Handbook (BALEAP 2022).

In mid-accreditation cycle, providers are invited to submit an interim review of accredited courses specifying how they have addressed recommendations and any substantial changes that have occurred since the accreditation visit, to ensure the provider remains in good standing.

In contrast to external examining which safeguards standards as evidenced through performance on assessed work, BALEAP accreditation looks more holistically at the provision, offering comments and making recommendations about multiple interlinked aspects. While external examiners draw on their subject expertise and knowledge about assessment scholarship when making evaluative judgement, assessors for the BALEAP course accreditation scheme spend some time observing how the provision is enacted in the classroom, how it fits within the context of the subject discipline within that particular institution and what measures it takes to develop in response to changing needs; how it achieves constructive alignment of outcomes, learning and assessment in response to clearly articulated principles and/or theory; and how collaboration is enacted, for the benefit of students, among academic literacies practitioners, subject discipline academics and other relevant colleagues within the institution.

External examiners' relationship with an institution develops over the four-year duration of their appointment as they gain an increased understanding of the context in which they are examining. The four-year timespan also allows examiners to evaluate the extent to which their recommendations have been successfully implemented, to fine-tune the way they frame recommendations and to prompt iterative cycles of reflection within the academic team delivering the course that they examine. External examiners are given access to documentation produced on a business-as-usual basis as part of the delivery of a course. They attend annual briefings run by the institution where they examine on any changes in regulations and processes. Assessment boards which include multiple courses are opportunities to learn from other examiners' comments and develop a broader contextual understanding. BALEAP accreditation visits, on the other hand, take place once every four years (with an interim reporting requirement). They require more complex curation of documentation which involves course teams in explicit reflection on the tacit knowledge and assumptions underpinning the design and delivery of the provision they put forward for accreditation and on the way evaluation of the provision is carried out. Due to its emphasis on contextualisation, constructive alignment and collaboration, the accreditation process aims to prompt collaborative sense-making and reflection among the course team as well as dialogue between course team members and other relevant functional areas (academic-related or professional services) within the institution where the provision is located. The BALEAP accreditation scheme has a set of criteria which help structure the reflective conversation. Evaluative comments are made by BALEAP assessors against each criterion, with explicit recommendations for action where applicable. The specific way in which recommendations are implemented, however, is the responsibility of the provider to establish and own.

Both approaches to quality assurance discussed in this section involve the use of expertise external to the provider institution, and both are a form of peer review, given that external examiners and BALEAP assessors have experience of working in comparable roles to the course team members for similar providers. Academic literacies practitioners do not have scope to influence the format of the evaluation. What they do have scope to influence, however, is the quality of the data put forward to support evaluative judgements as well as owning the solutions developed in response to suggestions and recommendations.

A Note on Making Quality and Impact Part and Parcel of the Natural Rhythm of an Institution

A key message the volume puts forward is the need for balance in resourcing quality assurance and enhancement activity. Balance needs to be achieved between formal, regulatory quality requirements endorsed above institution level and context-specific evaluative practices that align to the specific priorities of an institution with regard to the learning journeys of its international students. Balance also needs to be achieved between effort expended on measuring and evaluating impact on the one hand and the perceived benefits of the enhancements implemented on the other.

Quality-focused practices should be viewed as integral to learning and teaching; building learning and teaching capacity within an institution and building quality evaluation capacity should be integrated. There is scope for practitioners to work collaboratively with educational research specialists and with data professionals within an institution to generate relevant insights. Institution-internal evaluation processes offer more scope for ownership: practitioners play an active role in establishing what is evaluated, what criteria should be applied and what the standards are. Practitioners design the format of the evaluation. They are able to use alternative formats to capture data about course quality and impact; allowing students to choose the focus and format of accounts, and, where relevant, tying these into academic study so that evaluation feels less like a disconnected activity and is likely to yield higher-quality information about course quality. External evaluation processes and criteria are predefined, yet in institutions with a mature quality culture these processes and criteria are used as part of enhancement conversations which lead to impactful learning experiences. Quality processes are made as transparent as possible and all stakeholders (international students included) understand and engage in them, drawing on (and where necessary reframing) the "cultural scripts" they bring with regard to quality from previous educational experiences.

Institutions with a mature quality culture are suitably aware of the audiences of an evaluation process and of how to present evaluation outcomes in a way that helps each of these audiences reach an informed decision, particularly but not only in situations where complex numeric data is involved. They view changes in data reporting requirements from external bodies as opportunities to integrate more fully the datasets they collect and to explore new ways to generate meaningful insights. The more mature the quality culture, the stronger position organisations are in to support international student experiences more holistically and to use the evidence available to develop more relevant curricula and university learning experiences. Mature quality cultures develop over time, with designated quality roles being identified in an institution, and with quality practices made as transparent and participatory as possible. Developing a mature quality culture within a higher education institution is crucial to delivering high-quality, impact-full learning and is particularly relevant in the current circumstances, where partnerships between higher education institutions globally are intensifying to facilitate life-relevant collaborative learning opportunities (e.g. British Council 2021).

References

Advance HE (2019) *External examining*. Advance HE https://www.advance-he.ac.uk/knowledge-hub/external-examining

Arkoudis, S. (2014) *Integrating English language communication skills into disciplinary curricula: Options and strategies*. Sydney: Office for Learning and Teaching http://www.cshe.unimelb.edu.au/research/teaching/docs/Arkoudis_S_NST_report_2014.pdf

BALEAP (2022) *BALEAP accreditation scheme (BAS) handbook*. BALEAP https://www.baleap.org/wp-content/uploads/2022/03/BAS-Accreditation-Hbook-v9x.pdf

Blaj-Ward, L. (2017a) *Language learning and use in English-medium higher education*. Palgrave Macmillan.

Blaj-Ward, L. (2017b) From language learner to language user in English-medium higher education: Language development brokers outside the language classroom. *Journal of Research in International Education*, 16(1): 55–64. https://doi.org/10.1177/1475240917694109

Blaj-Ward, L. (2020) *Making external examining fit for the future*. Advance HE https://www.advance-he.ac.uk/news-and-views/making-external-examining-fit-future

British Council (2021) *Role of international higher education partnerships in contributing to the sustainable development goals*. British Council https://www.britishcouncil.org/sites/default/files/role_of_international_higher_education_partnerships_in_contributing_to_the_sustainable_development_goals.pdf

Evans, S., & B. Morrison (2012) Learning and using English at university: Lessons from a longitudinal study in Hong Kong. *The Journal of Asia TEFL*, 9(2): 21–47. http://journal.asiatefl.org/

Hoareau McGrath, C., B. Guerin, E. Harte, M. Frearson, & C. Manville (2015) *Learning gain in higher education*. RAND Corporation https://www.rand.org/pubs/research_reports/RR996.html

Humphreys, P., M. Haugh, B. Fenton-Smith, A. Lobo, R. Michael, & I. Walkinshaw (2012) Tracking international students' English proficiency over the first semester of undergraduate study. *IELTS Research Reports Online Series*, 2012(1): 1–41. https://www.ielts.org/teaching-and-research/research-reports/online-series-2012-1

Kandiko Howson, C. (2019) *Final evaluation of the office for students learning gain pilot projects*. Office for Students. https://www.officeforstudents.org.uk/media/20ffe802-9482-4f55-b5a0-6c18ee4e01b1/learning-gain-project-final-evaluation.pdf

Kandiko Howson, C., & A. Buckley (2020) Quantifying learning: Measuring student outcomes in higher education in England. *Politics and Governance*, 8(2): 6–14. https://doi.org/10.17645/pag.v8i2.2564

Mercado, S., & L. Gibson (2013) *The key elements of transnational education (TNE)*. EAIE https://www.eaie.org/blog/key-elements-transnational-education-tne.html

Murray, N. (2016) *Standards of English in higher education*. Cambridge University Press.

Neubauer, D.E., & C. Gomes (2017) *Quality assurance in Asia-Pacific universities: Implementing massification in higher education*. Palgrave.

Nguyen, C.H., & M. Shah (2019) *Quality assurance in Vietnamese higher education: Policy and practice in the 21st century*. Palgrave Macmillan.

Oliver, R., S. Vanderford, & E. Grote (2012) Evidence of English language proficiency and academic achievement of non-English speaking background students. *Higher Education Research and Development*, 31(4): 541–555. https://doi.org/10.1080/07294360.2011.653958

Pearson, W.S. (2020) The effectiveness of pre-sessional EAP programmes in UK higher education: A review of the evidence. *Review of Education*, 8(2): 420–447. https://doi.org/10.1002/rev3.3191

QAA (2021a) *Country report: United Arab Emirates*. QAA https://www.qaa.ac.uk/international/country-reports

QAA (2021b) *Country reports: Japan*. QAA https://www.qaa.ac.uk/international/country-reports

Rahnuma, N. (2020) Evolution of quality culture in an HEI: Critical insights from university staff in Bangladesh. *Educational Assessment, Evaluation and Accountability*, 32: 53–81. https://doi.org/10.1007/s11092-019-09313-8

Rosa, M.J., & A. Amaral (2014) *Quality assurance in higher education: Contemporary debates*. Palgrave.

Rosa, M.J., C.S. Sarrico, O. Tavares, & A. Amaral (2016) *Cross-border higher education and quality assurance: Commerce, the services directive and governing higher education*. Palgrave Macmillan.

Saunders, M. (2011) Setting the scene: The four domains of evaluative practice in higher education. In M. Saunders, P. Trowler & V. Bamber (Eds.). *Reconceptualising evaluation in higher education: The practice turn* (pp. 1–17). Open University Press.

Saunders, M., P. Trowler, & V. Bamber (Eds.). (2011) *Reconceptualising evaluation in higher education: The practice turn*. Open University Press.

Storch, N., & K. Hill (2008) What happens to international students' English after one semester at university? *Australian Review of Applied Linguistics*, 31(1): 04.1–04.17. https://doi.org/10.2104/aral0804

TEQSA (2020) *Guidance note: Monitoring and analysis of student performance.* TEQSA https://www.teqsa.gov.au/latest-news/publications/guidance-note-monitoring-and-analysis-student-performance

Tight, M. (2021) Existing research on learning gain in higher education. In C. Hughes & M. Tight (Eds.). *Learning gain in higher education* (pp. 1–17). Emerald Publishing Limited.

Trifiro, F. (2021) How a misplaced attention to the student experience can limit the progressive impact of TNE. In V. Tsiligiris, W. Lawton & C. Hill (Eds.). *Importing transnational education capacity, sustainability and student experience from the host country perspective* (pp. 237–249). Palgrave Macmillan.

Zozimo, J. (2020) What if evaluation takes place seated around the table whilst enjoying a drink? A social practice view of evaluation of development education. *Journal of International Development*, 32: 302–323. https://doi.org/10.1002/jid.3439

CHAPTER 3

Experiencing Impact and Quality: International Student Journeys

Opening Section

The nature of the processes that underpin external benchmarking of quality and impact in higher education, discussed in the previous chapter, inevitably means that the detail of international student lived experiences is decontextualised, if not fully erased, from formal quality and impact reports. However, it is the rich detail of individual experiences that offers the most valuable insights to practitioners looking to enhance academic literacies provision for the benefit of their students. Student lived experiences are the focus of the present chapter.

The vignette which opens the volume captures just one of a myriad of journeys that international students undertake across national boundaries (with or without actual physical mobility). Kay, the Graphic Design student in the vignette, will experience the quality and impact of academic literacies provision in an emergency remote teaching context in a way that is unique to her, and it is the personalised nature of provision that will help Kay nurture her hopes and reach her full potential. However, there are some core elements of quality and impact that cut across all experiences. The present chapter aims to capture both the uniqueness and the shared elements of international students' university experiences.

The qualitative research I conducted in the five years before the pandemic, with international students who made the physical journey to the

L. Blaj-Ward, *Academic Literacies Provision for International Students*, https://doi.org/10.1007/978-3-031-11503-5_3

UK to study for an undergraduate or postgraduate degree, helped me develop a fuller understanding of how these students grew into competent, confident communicators in an academic environment. Their learning journeys were not necessarily linear success stories but their experiences—in scheduled academic literacies sessions or when seeking informal support—provided a lens through which to evaluate the allocation and effective use of academic literacies resource. In the present chapter, I revisit the insights from my previous publications and contextualise discussion within a synthesis of relevant, recently published literature in the field. My reflection on how my own practice changed in response to a global pandemic also informs discussion. I offer three scenarios which focus on the student perspective through a qualitative lens:

- Student-led evaluation of academic literacies provision focused on a specific assessed piece of work
- An evaluation process that explores connections between academic literacies and students' aspirations with regard to careers and life more broadly beyond graduation
- Opportunities for students to co-create academic literacies provision, inputting into the enhancement process as active participants.

Each vignette is accompanied by a number of questions I invite the readers to consider. These are questions that could be asked so that international students' voices feed more fully into the design and development of academic literacies provision as well as so that participation in the evaluation process itself is an additional opportunity for learning.

Exploring International Student Experiences of Academic Literacies Provision at University

In my first substantial contribution to the body of knowledge related to how international students experience academic literacies provision at university, a desktop mapping of academic literature and professional debates filtered through my own experience as a practitioner (Blaj-Ward 2014). I included a chapter on "Researching student participation in the EAP setting". That chapter opens with a consideration of needs analysis, a core practice adopted when designing academic literacies provision that puts students at the centre, meets good practice expectations and is therefore likely to impact positively on the student academic experience (see also Basturkmen 2020; Brown 2016). A comprehensive needs analysis process covers three core aspects. One is the literacies students need to be familiar with in order to be successful on their course. Another is the distance to be travelled between students' English language proficiency prior to the start of the course and the level required to meet the course learning outcomes. The third but equally important aspect to consider encompasses students' own goals and expectations about the academic literacies provision made available to them.

My experience as a practitioner up to that point had made me acutely aware that student goals and expectations have a substantial influence on how students engage with formal academic literacies provision—and that provision focusing solely on unpacking features of the target context was unlikely to engage them fully or lead to expected results. It became clear to me that constructive alignment between intended learning outcomes, learning activities and assessment, as conceptualised by Biggs and Tang (2011), should include an additional loop to individual student goals and space for learning to happen in unplanned ways. Biggs and Tang (2011) do make allowance for unintended learning outcomes in their discussion of constructive alignment. From an academic literacies point of view, however, what counts as "unintended" from a course designer perspective has a more central place in the learning experience and needs equally careful scaffolding, along the lines of the negotiated syllabus approach described by Macalister (2015) among others. A negotiated syllabus allows students to make important choices about what and how they want to learn and enables the development of student autonomy and lifelong learning habits. It also allows them to bring into the academic literacies setting knowledge they have about literacies appropriate in different domains of life and to appreciate how these complement each other.

The literature I reviewed for the Blaj-Ward (2014) volume provided underpinning evidence of the importance of making needs analysis an ongoing concern, given that students' goals and expectations are likely to change as they progress through their course. The process of synthesising insights from the literature offered an opportunity to reflect on how to balance various considerations related to needs analysis such as the desire to use creative methodologies to arrive at rich, complex needs information; the practical and ethical considerations about the time and effort students are required to put into the needs analysis process; the staff resource available (in terms of time and expertise); and the extent to which enhancements based on needs data are likely to have a positive impact on students' learning experience. The mapping exercise also revealed a body of literature not previously referenced in the context of discussions about academic literacies provision, but with high relevance, namely language learning and use in study abroad (e.g. Kinginger 2009).

The study abroad literature explores the learning that happens as a result of immersion in a context where a language is used extensively for a variety of communication purposes. A particular thread stood out for me, and I built on this in subsequent research. The thread relates to the distinction between language learner and language user (Benson et al. 2014), and the identity shift students experience when they transition from engaging with English language as an object of study in the formal and ultimately artificial context of the language classroom to making use of the language in the context of studying for a university degree. The shift impacts on the way students interact with others in the setting and on their ability to build meaningful relationships that support their learning and growth. Academic literacies provision is one of several contexts which have the potential to facilitate the transition from learner to user. Provision caters for a range of international students with varying degrees of English language proficiency and also varies in terms of the extent to which it integrates attention to language. An explicit focus on language may impact on how students perceive the relevance and quality of the provision, engage with it and experience its intended benefits. Students who had not had positive experiences of learning English in a language classroom within the formal education system (e.g. Sakui and Cowie 2008) were more likely to engage with provision that was presented to them not as an opportunity for language development but as a context in which to unpack expectations related to academic tasks. Gurney (2016) offers additional nuance to the conversation, through a useful reminder that even where interactions take place in a national context where English is the language spoken outside campus gates, in the narrower context in which interactions unfold on campus the students may be using English as a lingua franca with non-native speakers in a sometimes substantially larger proportion than native ones. Value judgements about what is acceptable English and the way in which English is perceived as a native language, as an additional language or as a lingua franca, are tied in with identity work and may act as enablers or conversely as barriers to student engagement in learning interactions.

Taking Benson et al. (2014) as a point of departure, I conducted a piece of research with 21 postgraduate students towards the end of a one-year course in the UK (Blaj-Ward 2017b). In one-off interviews, I explored with students the situations in which they found themselves communicating, how they maximised their participation in English-medium higher education contexts and what helped them build themselves up as fully functioning participants in a higher education context, making the transition from language learner to language user. I used the concept of language development brokers, reframing Lillis and Curry's (2010) "literacy brokers" to make sense of the experiences shared with me. I learnt that my interviewees drew on a range of language development brokers, beyond their academic literacies tutors, and experienced greater development when they had access to social relationships in situations in which they were perceived as valued partners in communication. Insights from the research prompted me to put forward a case that all stakeholders in EMI contexts, not just language and academic literacies tutors, should be sensitised to the importance of language development brokering in supporting non-native speakers in English-medium higher education contexts. The research helped me reframe the way I explained the purpose of academic literacies provision to students in my day-to-day teaching practice. It prompted me to rethink questions I asked my students about their goals, expectations and language learner histories to inform provision design. It helped shape conversations with colleagues in a range of academic and other professional roles about international student support.

Insights from the Blaj-Ward (2017b) interviews resonated with my day-to-day practice, and I chose to build on these in subsequent research, to understand more fully students' perspective on academic literacies provision. The article put the spotlight firmly on student experiences, as did *Language Learning and Use in English Medium Higher Education* (Blaj-Ward 2017a). A later article I co-authored with a colleague (Blaj-Ward and Matic 2020) provided an opportunity to go one step further, shifting the focus from language development to overall academic experiences. To be able to evaluate the impact of my practice more fully, and to be in a stronger position to offer guidance on others' practice, it became apparent that I would need to explore, from the students' perspective, how they engage with academic assessments that have relevance for their career aspirations beyond university. The article was premised on the view, supported by Ajjawi et al. (2020) among others, that assessment

> is central to university experience as it focuses students' attention and encourages them to select areas of the curriculum with which to engage in

> more depth, impacting not only on the outcome of the specific assessment event but also on their sense of self-efficacy and their awareness of new levels to which they can take their passion for learning and their aspirations for the future. (Blaj-Ward and Matic 2020, p. 2)

The interviewees revealed the diverse criteria they used to select personally relevant examples of "assessment for employability learning" (Boud and Ajjawi 2019; Jorre de St Jorre and Oliver 2018) and the complex learning interactions they engaged in to complete those assessments in ways that were meaningful to them. Looked at through the lenses of careers theory, pre-professional identity and possible selves, they justify a recommendation that assessment design and the scaffolding of assessment experiences (even ones without an explicit workplace or work-like experience component) should call on a broader range of experts (e.g. alumni, business stakeholders and members of civic organisations, as well as technicians or careers professionals) as equal partners, to achieve the desired quality and impact.

Academic literacies practitioners are an additional set of partners with valuable expertise in assessment design as well as in the design of learning and teaching experiences more broadly. Carefully designed academic literacies provision which aims for maximum impact wraps itself around the academic core of university experiences. When students enrol on a university course in a different country, and relocate physically or virtually for that purpose, they do so motivated by a wide array of dreams, hopes and aspirations that go beyond academic success. Academic literacies provision does play a part in the achievement of dreams, hopes and aspirations, and in order to fully understand its value and impact from the point of view of students, for academic and life success, it is essential to explore its connections with the broader student experience, given the increasingly porous boundaries between academic settings and the wider world outside academic campus gates. Indeed, Robertson et al. (2011) highlight the "complexity of interdependence" between the various aspects which international students take into consideration to make decisions on long-term goals associated with an academic degree course ("work and career, financial security, home ownership, travel, personal development and overall life-satisfaction", p. 691). The level of priority assigned by students to these aspects will influence the way they engage with their course overall and the expectations they have for academic literacies provision in particular.

The pandemic which swept the world in early 2020 caused substantial disruption to physical geographic mobility. The geographically uneven evolution of the pandemic meant that even where mobility did occur, scenarios such as the one described by Maloney and Kim (2020), with students in residence learning virtually, were still possible. In-person interaction was replaced by synchronous online communication, which added a layer of complexity to the literacies that students needed to develop. The added complexity spanned the practicalities of using digital technologies; the skills to display information multimodally joining visual and aural information with written text as seamlessly as possible across sections of an online environment; new lexical resource and functional language to manage virtual interaction; and, equally important, digital citizenship, enabling students to "participate fully and appropriately in the broad range of social and professional digital communities available to them" (Blaj-Ward and Winter 2019, p. 880).

Three complementary scenarios are included in this chapter, exploring student perspectives on how academic literacies provision in a higher education context shaped by the pandemic scaffolds their development as competent communicators and (digital) citizens. The first focuses on student engagement with academic assessment within the curriculum, linking quality and impact to student academic achievement and satisfaction and asking whether a broader framing of quality and impact is possible and useful for academic literacies practitioners to consider. The second scenario looks at impact more broadly, considering not academic learning as such but student aspirations beyond graduation with regard to careers and life. The third addresses co-creation: the opportunity for students to actively engage in designing and delivering academic literacies provision, going a step further than having their voice represented through feedback collection or in student committees.

Scenario 1 of 3: Student-Led Evaluation of Assignment-Focused Academic Literacies Provision

A substantial proportion of academic literacies provision is aligned to university assignments and scaffolding students' experience of completing summatively assessed work. In these cases, impact is frequently framed in terms of grades obtained and student satisfaction with the delivery of the provision.

Consider the following scenario:

On Lucy's timetable (MSc Human Resource Management), a new session has appeared, a couple of weeks before her assignment submission deadline, with an academic literacies focus. The assignment is an annotated interview. In groups of four or five, the students on Lucy's course have each interviewed an employee of a medium-sized company about challenges they've experienced with accessing relevant professional development opportunities, and, using insights from background reading, they are expected to annotate the interviews and then combine their knowledge to develop recommendations to the company. The academic literacies session is designed to help students explore how to frame and word annotations so that they bring out fully the value of the evidence collected through the interviews. In the session, the tutor shares examples of annotated interview excerpts and asks the students to compare them and evaluate their potential effectiveness. The students then draft and share the annotations for excerpts from their own interviews, for peer feedback. Appropriate use of quality background reading is one of the assessment criteria. After the session, Lucy receives an email with a link to a brief form which invites her to feed back on the session. Lucy chooses a score of 5 out of 5, uploads a drawing of a smiley face and adds the following comment:

I very much enjoyed participating in the discussion and the examples of annotations were very clear, but perhaps future students would benefit from having this session earlier because it would help guide their thinking around interview questions and help them get better quality interview data on which to make richer annotations. Some of the students on the course found it difficult to get enough information because they didn't know enough about the company and weren't sure how to ask good questions. They would also have benefited from having their questions checked for language accuracy and from guidance on how to ask follow-on questions.

Was the session sufficiently impactful for Lucy? Did it help her produce a better assignment? Did it teach her anything useful about interaction in a workplace context when interviewing employees? Were there any unintended but valuable learning outcomes? In the first instance, this very much depends on how closely the designer of the academic literacies session has interacted with the team who have developed and will be grading the assignment; how much understanding the session designer has of the process the students need to go through to in order to arrive at a successful outcome; and what aspects of the assignment the students could potentially find challenging. An understanding of the assignment genre is essential—both the written output to be produced and the interaction through which students gather and process relevant material. At the delivery stage, it depends on whether Lucy has had sufficient opportunity in the session (or in a follow-on one-to-one meeting) to explore the information shared and calibrate her understanding of expectations. At the stage where Lucy is completing the assignment, emphasis shifts to how ready Lucy is to apply her new understanding of assignment expectations. At the stage where Lucy receives feedback on the graded assignment, she will be in a position to reflect on how successfully she has applied her learning from the academic literacies session and on what aspects she would have benefited from additional or different guidance.

To gauge the quality and impact of the academic literacies session, there are various questions that Lucy and her peers could be invited to answer—at various stages in their experience. From the standpoint of the programme team and institution, the level of resource to gather and process data will have a bearing on the size of the data gathering and processing activity, as will the perceived benefit of this. From the perspective of the students, gauging quality and impact could in itself be a way to generate additional impact. For example, the form in the scenario further above is anonymous but if it had the option for students to add their name—and Lucy did add hers—students could receive a thank-you note for the useful suggestions made, which they could add to a portfolio of achievements and gain some form of credit for. Feeding back in this instance is both a form of quality assurance and an opportunity for students to learn and grow. Going one step further, for a future iteration of the academic literacies session, consideration could be given to engaging students in the design of the evaluation tools—the questions they feel would be useful for them to answer, the point in their learning journey where they feel they could best offer feedback and the medium through which this could most effectively be done.

Student feedback offers insights into their experience which session designers will then draw on to fine-tune provision, to ensure that future learning experiences are scaffolded more fully. The way questions are framed to elicit feedback influences what information students choose to share about the extent to which they found the learning experience rewarding. To what extent was Lucy's learning experience rewarding? One thing that Lucy does not mention in the feedback form—because the question is not asked directly and Lucy is unsure whether this would be appropriate to share because it feels less academic—is how valuable she found the opportunity to talk to an actual company employee. The interview took place in the shared kitchen space of the medium-sized company. The interviewee made Lucy a cup of tea, patiently waited for Lucy to frame her questions, appreciated that Lucy might be slightly apprehensive about making mistakes and generously offered insights into the range of forms of professional development she had had the opportunity to engage in in a variety of contexts or was planning to explore. For Lucy, the assignment was not simply a piece of academic work she had to complete but an experience which generated wellbeing, relevant learning of how to build a sustainable career (in terms of immediate steps and longer-term goals) and validation of her ability to use English effectively in a real-life context.

Neither the MSc Human Resource Management module feedback form nor the feedback form for the flexibly designed academic literacies session capture these aspects of Lucy's experience. The annotations that students are required to make are oriented towards developing recommendations for the company, and there is no requirement for students to reflect on their personal learning from the interview. The needs analysis the academic literacies tutor conducted prior to designing the session focused on academic needs closely aligned to a specific assignment rather than looking at whole person development or at how the assignment fits into the broader course strategy.

Lucy's experience raises several questions from a quality and impact point of view:

- How could student feedback processes be redesigned to capture valuable incidental learning in addition to general student satisfaction data?
- How does a more pragmatic framing of the purpose of the academic literacies session (i.e. supporting students with completing a discrete piece of assessed work and focusing on features of academic writing) sit alongside a broader understanding of assessment for learning and assessment as learning (QAA and Advance HE 2021; Nicol and Macfarlane-Dick 2006)?
- How can academic literacies provision be made more integral to the course so that it reflects more fully the need for assessment to be authentic, that is, "the ways in which assessment does, or does not, enable individual student fulfilment and a sense of self" (McArthur 2021, p. 6)—beyond more narrowly defined academic learning?

- Will the company receiving recommendations from Lucy have an opportunity to respond to the recommendations, closing a loop and generating additional learning impact for Lucy?
- How much involvement will the academic literacies tutor have in the giving and receiving of feedback between Lucy and the company where Lucy carries out the interview and makes CPD recommendations for? How will that feedback be captured and processed for quality enhancement purposes?
- What support would Lucy and others in her position need to lead post-assignment debrief activity and capture useful insights into broader aspects of the assessment experience?
- Which stage/s of the formal quality assurance cycle that courses go through at Lucy's institution would be the most appropriate one to document insights and actions that arise in response to student-led feedback on quality and impact? Should these insights be channelled through formal student course representative roles only? To what extent are students involved in implementing the action points?

Scenario 2 of 3: Impact Beyond Course Completion

Lucy's experience of completing an assignment which has tangible impact beyond the campus walls and which contributes to Lucy's growth in confidence as a professional in her field resonates with the recent emphasis, in a globally engaged higher education sector, on developing international student readiness for work and life (e.g. HEPI 2021; Coelen and Gribble 2019).

With specific reference to the UK, the HEPI (2021) report notes:

> Over the past 10 years or so, UK higher education providers have placed employability more prominently within their offer to students, increasingly embedding employability-related learning within the curriculum (although the extent varies by subject) in addition to providing discrete career support services to students. The UK offer places emphasis on the value of extracurricular opportunities that build student experiences and contribute to a strong CV. Schemes and awards within individual universities to recognise these aspects of learning have proliferated.
>
> Yet the actual experiences of international students in relation to career and employability support while at UK universities have been under-researched. One recent report on supporting international graduate employability in the UK, based on the views of careers professionals, questions

whether careers services currently have the capacity to support international students. The same research shows that, while many universities do provide some information to students about working outside the UK, around half do not provide tailored support to international students while a substantial minority cannot meet the demand from them (UUK International 2020). (HEPI 2021, pp. 53–54)

The HEPI report focuses on international students' experience of specialist careers services and extracurricular opportunities; however, readiness for work and life is also supported through the taught curriculum, as highlighted in various studies reviewed in Advance HE (2021). Through the curriculum, there is scope for academic literacies provision to make an overt contribution to cultivating international student employability.

To gain broader perspective on how international students' employability learning can be scaffolded more fully, the HEPI (2021) report should be read alongside Huang and Curle (2021), a recent piece of research which adds value to a discussion of impact beyond degree course completion. In an EMI context, Huang and Curle (2021) explored Chinese students' perceptions of the link between higher education medium of instruction and career prospects. Although not referring specifically to the academic literacies component within the EMI Finance programme, the research holds in full awareness the impact of the language of instruction on students' depth of engagement with the academic content as well as its relationship to students' (future) career prospects. The research respondents (50 undergraduate students towards the end of their academic journey and 50 alumni of the same programme with at least six months' post-graduation employment experience) shared their perceptions of EMI and career prospects and their evaluation of the EMI experience they were undergoing or, in the case of alumni, had completed. Language-focused provision was frontloaded in the first two years of the undergraduate journey, restricting the time available for students to engage with substantive content knowledge and therefore, in their view, their ability to acquire a sufficiently in-depth understanding of their chosen subject. At the same time, the content delivered in English appeared not to be sufficiently aligned to the chosen subject, providing broader contextual knowledge rather than up-to-date specialist information required for professional accreditation or for progression onto a Chinese-medium postgraduate course. The EMI curriculum appeared to expand career options and to prepare students well for postgraduate study in an

English-speaking country but was perceived as somewhat less effective with regard to pursuing a career in China with major employers in the finance sector.

On the basis of their data, Huang and Curle (2021) advise re-evaluating curriculum design overall and emphasise that "[a]ny HEI implementing EMI should therefore prioritise student opinions, feedback and EMI programme evaluation to then take action to improve their EMI programmes" (p. 340). Ensuring that students and alumni play an active role in initial curriculum design and ongoing enhancement is crucial to the success of a course. Given the strong needs analysis base on which it is built, academic literacies provision can serve as a model for an ongoing process of course re-evaluation and enhancement focused on achieving impact beyond course completion, as illustrated in the vignette below:

One of the modules on Amber's course centres on a group project. Students work collaboratively, in teams of four or five, to develop a solution to a climate-related issue. This is a second-year undergraduate module offered to students from a cluster of different subject areas, and student learning is formally assessed via a group report and an individual reflection. The solution needs to be feasible but not necessarily fully implemented by the end of the module—the learning outcomes for the module recognise the constraints students work within. The aim is to encourage the development of communication skills and creative approaches to solution-finding. Teams are carefully chosen to include multiple backgrounds and levels or types of experience. Students take a test at the start of the course to identify their preferred team role and are asked to write a brief biography, used as a basis for selecting team members.

Built into the module is an academic literacies strand whose primary aim is to support report writing. The literacies strand does not have a separately assessed component. It soon becomes apparent, however, that the specific nature of the report makes it easy to be amply supported by the subject team and that the literacies strand would add value by focusing on communication and teamwork. The sessions use LinkedIn learning materials about aspects such as giving feedback, writing workplace emails, articulating one's strengths in cover letters for work experience applications or disagreeing constructively. An optional "assessment" for the module is a "To whom it may concern" recommendation letter, written by the academic literacies tutor on the basis of student progress throughout the module, their self-evaluation and a final reflective conversation between the student and the academic literacies tutor.

The assessment is optional but Amber completes all stages and subsequently makes successful use of the recommendation letter when applying for a work experience opportunity at the end of her second year.

The optional assessment developed by the academic literacies tutor has immediate, tangible impact in Amber's case. The literacies strand enables her to reflect on her communication approach and on her learning from the module. It helps her to articulate more fully and confidently her strengths and her willingness to continue to learn and develop—all important aspects of learning at university and beyond.

The literacies strand is evaluated through a separate feedback form, which includes, alongside student satisfaction questions, items that prompt additional reflection on learning, as follows:

> *Give an example of a situation when you were misunderstood during the module. How did you clarify the misunderstanding? What would have happened if you hadn't managed to sort things out?*
>
> *Give an example of a situation in which you listened patiently and carefully and appropriately acknowledged a team member's idea. What was the outcome of that situation?*
>
> *Give an example of a situation in which you had to build consensus while working on your project. What was the greatest difficulty and how did you overcome it? Why was consensus important?*
>
> *In which of the aspects below did you improve the most during the module? Please choose one aspect only and give a specific example from your experience.*

- *Ability to provide information in a clear and well-structured way in a variety of media*
- *Tailoring messages appropriately for different audiences*
- *Making effective use of visual material in communication*
- *Negotiating, persuading and influencing to ensure that projects have high quality outcomes and are delivered by set deadlines*
- *Communicating in a way that has a positive impact on other people.*

The literacies captured through the questions are relevant for university study as well as for life and work beyond university. The questions allow detail about (international) student experiences to be captured in a way that is relevant both for individual student learning and for module redesign to fit the needs of subsequent cohorts. The feedback form is completed prior to the final reflective conversation between the student and the academic literacies tutor. The main module assessment creates an experiential framework; the literacies strand scaffolds reflection on experience in order to develop employability.

The Amber vignette above is set in a face-to-face teaching context in a country where English is the main language spoken on campus and outside campus gates. Unprecedented circumstances created by the pandemic are still placing international student geographic mobility under a question mark. A vibrant international student community may take a while to develop on physical campuses in English-speaking countries. In the UK, the post-study visa for international students offers an additional incentive for international students to enrol on courses at UK universities. Not all geographically mobile students aspire to stay in the country where they studied. In the changed current and future labour market, however, regardless of physical geographic mobility, employability learning has acquired new urgency. Evidence of recent good practice in supporting international students' employability is available (UUK International 2020), and employability learning provision is responding to new ways of working in a digitally enhanced world. Academic literacies offers an ideal context in which to develop students' ability to communicate with confidence, clarity and care; to scaffold experiences of authentic, sustainable assessment; and to respond flexibly to new expectations about employability learning. It also offers an ideal context to explore how international students can most effectively be involved as equal partners in researching and designing employability-relevant learning experiences that benefit all students on campus, not just international ones, and lay the groundwork for meaningful academic learning which underpins sustainable careers.

Amber's experience raises several questions from a quality and impact point of view:

- How could the feedback form be integrated effectively into a group activity, facilitated in person or digitally, with participants supporting each other's reflection and learning more fully?
- How could collaborative group activity in the module Amber is taking be extended to include participants from universities based in other countries—therefore creating greater learning impact—and how could academic literacies provision unpack expectations about collaborative learning so that all participants feel included?
- What categories of stakeholders external to the course and university could be included in the evaluation of the solution to a climate-related issue, so that learning feels authentic to the students and has greater potential to generate impact beyond completing a piece of academic work?

Scenario 3 of 3: Co-creating Academic Literacies Provision with Students

Academic literacies provision which fully meets the needs of students enrolled on a university degree programme should ideally be designed in collaboration with the students themselves. Clarifying expectations from the start with regard to the focus and format of the provision and the responsibilities of the various stakeholders involved in the provision will help ensure the course is of the highest quality. Giving students ownership and agency within the process of designing provision creates opportunities for deeper engagement. Ownership and agency start with co-creating learning outcomes for the academic literacies sessions—while practitioners bring prior understanding of the literacies students need to be familiar with in order to be successful on their main subject course, it is the students who need to establish the distance they are prepared to travel between the start and end of the subject course to meet the learning outcomes officially approved by the institution. When outcomes have been established, resources and, if applicable, assessments can be co-created.

An example of co-creating resources is offered below:

Kay, the student in the vignette which opens this volume, has been encouraged to access self-study resources in the library to develop her confidence in writing academically. One of the volumes on the self-study shelf is Crème and Lea's *(2007)* Writing at University: A Guide for Students. *Kay's specialism is graphic design, and academic writing is not one of her perceived strengths. Although Kay appreciates the importance of reading about how the graphic design field has developed, her preference is for texts which combine verbal and visual elements into a coherent whole. Words have deeper, richer meanings for Kay if she can connect them to images, however tenuous those connections can sometimes appear to be. Kay attempts to engage with Crème and Lea's text; she does find useful insights but struggles a bit to apply them. Serendipitously, as an extracurricular project, Kay is given the opportunity to work alongside an academic literacies member of staff to develop a "Colouring book for writing: A designer's guide to colouring-in a literature review". The academic literacies practitioner has conducted a piece of small-scale, exploratory research into how design students engage with academic writing tasks and would like guidance on how to help students explore and appreciate more fully the similarities between the design process and the way academic writing takes shape.*

Lea (2016) writes the following about her co-authored volume *Writing at University: A Guide for Students* (Crème and Lea 2007):

Throughout the book we offered explanations and activities that contrasted with a deficit model, with its focus on student writing as problem. For example, there is significant attention paid to how assignments vary from one another. We reject a 'key words in the title' approach and ask the reader to analyse the title in a variety of discursive ways, suggesting that they write in some detail about the assignment and its preparation, with a dominant focus on their own understandings and experience. Readers are introduced to the idea that writing is not just an empty vessel carrying along subject or disciplinary context but integrally related to the ways in which different subjects and disciplines view the world. All the activities are contextualised and ask the reader to engage with these through their own university writing. (p. 91)

Lea is partly responding to the perceived risk of the book being read as proposing a more normative view of academic writing, not sufficiently aligned to the ethos of the signature Lea and Street (1998)-initiated academic literacies approach. The emphasis that "writing is not just an empty vessel carrying along subject or disciplinary context but integrally related to the ways in which different subjects and disciplines view the world" (Lea 2016, p. 91) is welcome but needs to be expanded to encompass more than just academic knowledge contained within closely delimited academic environments. Academic writing is a form of learning. Genuinely impactful and valuable learning at university goes beyond developing confident academic writer identities—it links to whole person development, wellbeing and meaningful contributions to communities and society.

Enhancing wellbeing is one of the aims of the project that Kay is engaging in. The academic literacies practitioner has shared with Kay highlights from her research. Together, they are planning a step-by-step guide to identifying and collating insights from the literature. The academic literacies practitioner's knowledge of writing processes and Kay's experience of design processes complement each other and offer a strong basis for the project to succeed. Kay also acts as a potential user, testing various iterations of the writing tasks and helping combine them into a workbook. Two tasks she enjoys the most are the initial key words one and the closing reflection. For the key words task, she designs three intricate key shapes with tags attached to which workbook users can add words that unlock the literature spaces where relevant information is held. She also prepares a couple of half-finished keys, one with an eye in the middle, linked to a quote about the mind's eye and visualising connections between ideas. Workbook users are invited to complete the half-finished keys; the drawing activity aims to enhance wellbeing but also to encourage users to establish their most important key word, the overarching, substantial concept which guides their engagement with the literature. The white space around the key shapes is there for additional notes to be made.

The academic literacies practitioner is keen to encourage students to reflect on the strategies that fill them up with writing energy and have the greatest impact on their ability to complete writing projects confidently. The visual Kay chooses for this is a tree surrounded by a circular bench. The tree crown has space for reflection notes. The bench invites workbook users to rest and reflect; the circular shape suggests that reflection should surround any activity so that it leads to meaningful growth. Reflection can be individual or it can be the outcome of a conversation—signified by the two dotted line silhouettes that Kay adds to the bench drawing.

Kay and the academic literacies practitioner test sections of the prototype workbook with several students who volunteer to help. Kay makes notes of their feedback—some of the volunteers are design students; others however draw for pleasure or do not identify themselves as keen on drawing at all. Student enthusiasm for the "colouring book for writing" varies but among the volunteers there is agreement that approaching the process in a more creative way pays dividends. An insight that a volunteer shares stays with Kay: one student mentions that he has no recollection of colouring books being used in his home or school context when he was growing up. The premise for the workbook was that students would tap into a form of visual literacy that was familiar and within their comfort zone (colouring), while developing one that they perceived as potentially more challenging (academic writing).

Each of the five workbook sections has an opening quote, to prompt reflection and connections. Kay and the academic literacies practitioner selected the quotes from a variety of source types, reflective of their own experience of finding inspiration in what sometimes appear to be the most unexpected of places and texts. While the academic literacies practitioner needs to convey, through the workbook, the rigour, thoroughness and systematic nature of academic research and scholarship, she also wants to capture the serendipitousness in the process, the joy of unplanned discoveries, the value of learning from various iterations of experience, in the less-structured curriculum spaces that Archer (2006) argues for in her academic literacies-informed work.

The workbook opens with the encouragement to "colour outside the lines, to be creative and confident in your academic writing, to choose a topic that really matters to you and makes a difference to others" and closes with an appendix that displays several different types of note paper style, so that students can be as creative as possible with the format of their notes, the colours, the fonts, the symbols they use, drawings and the way notes are laid out on the page. The workbook is designed to be used both as a paper copy to be printed and scribbled on and as a pdf that can be annotated digitally.

In Kay's case, the output to be co-created was suggested in advance by an academic literacies practitioner and was designed to be used with a different cohort. Co-creation, however, can focus on learning outcomes, to be agreed with the same cohort, similar in principle with Macalister's (2015) description of a negotiated syllabus.

Questions that could be asked with regard to co-creation are as follows.

- How much and what kind of scaffolding do students need in order to feel sufficiently confident to engage meaningfully in co-creation work in the context of academic literacies provision?
- How does co-creation align with the approach taken on the main subject course?
- What is the best balance between evaluating specific learning that links directly to assessed academic outcomes on a subject course and students' overall gain and development from the co-creation experience in the academic literacies context (when the latter may or may not be formally and explicitly captured in assessment criteria)?
- Would students benefit from seeing co-creation modelled by the course team—with staff from different functional areas (including academic literacies practitioners) working together and opening up relevant aspects of the collaboration process for scrutiny by students?
- How can parity of engagement in co-creation be ensured across whole cohorts so that the students who would benefit most from the provision shape the way in which the provision is designed—as opposed to the shaping being driven by the more confident communicators?

Closing Section

Understanding international student experiences of learning to communicate at university is fundamental to ensuring that academic literacies provision meets their needs. English for Academic Purposes literature discusses needs analysis at length, offering a range of options for practitioners to gather and process needs data. Academic literacies work provides additional nuance to the discussion of needs, by teasing out identity implications and the transformative experiences that students (arguably) undergo along their journey through an academic degree course.

Academic literacies work centres on personal growth and individual engagement (see, e.g. Burgess and Ivanič 2010). At the same time, it draws attention to the importance of taking an institutional viewpoint and highlights institutional responsibility to resource learning journeys through mainstreaming and embeddedness of provision. Differentiation of provision based on students' use of English as first, second, additional or foreign language has been problematised by authors such as Lillis and Tuck (2016), among others. The present volume supports this problematisation to a certain extent, but calls for attention to language proficiency to be integrated into the process of designing of the provision, given the wide variation in international student recruitment criteria across English-medium instruction courses globally (e.g. for recent discussion of the EMI landscape, see contributions to edited collections by Lasagabaster and Doiz 2021, and Su et al. 2021, respectively).

Academic literacies literature offers case studies of embedded provision but engages less explicitly or extensively than might be expected with evaluation from the student viewpoint, beyond comparing outcomes or looking at satisfaction data. Non-credit-bearing academic literacies provision is less constrained by formal quality assurance processes in an institution and involves greater scope for personalisation of the evaluation process to the individual and shared needs of specific cohorts. Arguably, this flexibility could help generate substantial positive impact on student learning. The absence of formal, institutionally sanctioned procedures to assure quality (e.g. an external examiner or the administration of a standard feedback questionnaire) does not necessarily result in lower-quality provision. Standard feedback questionnaires which institutions administer may not necessarily be the most appropriate way to capture the rich, complex learning that academic literacies provision prompts for international students, or the ripple effect that this learning generates in the longer term.

Two things stand out from the discussion in this chapter with regard to focusing on lived student experiences of quality and impact. One is that regardless of the provision type and timing, the overarching aims should be to enable communicating with confidence, clarity, and care. Confidence results from having a broad enough repertoire of communication strategies that can be flexibly adapted to suit different formats (e.g. a reflective report, a critical systematic synthesis of literature or a research interview) and having a range of tools at one's fingertips to explore the features of new communicative situations. Clarity refers to choosing the most relevant words and constructing sequences of ideas that can be understood with minimum processing effort for maximum impact. Care relates to making sure the communication has meaning, purpose and positive impact relevant for all participants in the communication (e.g. the material selected for a report covers the most relevant aspects and supports a balanced viewpoint, leading to increased knowledge and personal growth for the report writer and audience rather than being an artificial exercise in academic writing, and, where possible, inspires an intervention with tangible impact).

The other refers to co-creation and its potential to lead to more impactful provision. Discussion of negotiated syllabi (Macalister 2015) mentions the need to scaffold students' engagement in negotiation. The same applies to co-creation of outcomes, resources or assessment. Kay's involvement in co-creating the colouring book for academic writing is driven by a keen interest in combining the visual and the verbal, and it is framed as an extracurricular opportunity that gives her additional employability capital. Scaling up co-creation to include larger numbers of students and placing it within the curriculum can only achieve the impact it is designed to have if the participation of students less likely to engage is supported and encouraged.

References

Advance HE (2021) *Employability: A review of the literature 2016–2021*. Advance HE https://www.advance-he.ac.uk/knowledge-hub/employability-review-literature-2016-2021

Ajjawi, R., J. Tai, T. L. H. Nghia, D. Boud, L. Johnson, & C.-J. Patrick (2020) Aligning assessment with the needs of work-integrated learning: The challenges of authentic assessment in a complex context. *Assessment & Evaluation in Higher Education*, 45(2): 304–316. https://doi.org/10.1080/0260293 8.2019.1639613

Archer, A. (2006) A multimodal approach to academic literacy practices: Problematising the visual/verbal divide. *Language and Education*, 20(6): 449–462. https://doi.org/10.2167/le677.0

Basturkmen, H. (2020) Needs analysis and syllabus design for language for specific purposes. In C. A. Chapelle (Ed.). *The concise encyclopedia of applied linguistics* (pp. 836–842). John Wiley & Sons.

Benson, P., G. Barkhuizen, P. Bodycott, & J. Brown (2014) *Second language identity in narratives of study abroad.* Palgrave.

Biggs, J. B., & C. S. K. Tang (2011) *Teaching for quality learning at university* (4th ed.). Open University Press.

Blaj-Ward, L. (2014) *Researching contexts, practices and pedagogies in English for Academic Purposes.* Palgrave Macmillan.

Blaj-Ward, L. (2017a) *Language learning and use in English-medium higher education.* Palgrave Macmillan.

Blaj-Ward, L. (2017b) From language learner to language user in English-medium higher education: Language development brokers outside the language classroom. *Journal of Research in International Education,* 16(1): 55–64. https://doi.org/10.1177/1475240917694109

Blaj-Ward, L., & J. Matic (2020) Navigating assessed coursework to build and validate professional identities: The experiences of fifteen international students in the UK. *Assessment & Evaluation in Higher Education,* 46(2): 326–337. https://doi.org/10.1080/02602938.2020.1774505

Blaj-Ward, L., & K. Winter (2019) Engaging students as digital citizens. *Higher Education Research & Development,* 38(5): 879–892. https://doi.org/10.1080/07294360.2019.1607829

Boud, D., & R. Ajjawi (2019) The place of student assessment in pursuing employability. In J. Higgs, W. Letts & G. Crisp (Eds.). *Education for employability (Volume 2): Learning for future possibilities* (pp. 167–178). Brill.

Brown, J.D. (2016) *Introducing needs analysis and English for Specific Purposes.* Routledge.

Burgess, A., & R. Ivanič (2010) Writing and being written: Issues of identity across timescales. *Written Communication,* 27(2): 228–255. https://doi.org/10.1177/0741088310363447

Coelen, R., & C. Gribble (Eds.). (2019) *Internationalization and employability in higher education.* Routledge.

Crème, P., & M. Lea (2007) *Writing at university: A guide for students* (3rd ed.). Open University Press.

Gurney, L. (2016) Challenges for developing EAP practice in Anglophone contexts. In I. Liyanage & B. Nima (Eds.). *Multidisciplinary research perspectives in education: Shared experiences from Australia and China* (pp. 7–16). Sense Publishers.

HEPI (2021) *Paying more for less? Careers and employability support for international students at UK universities.* HEPI Report 143 https://www.hepi.ac.uk/wp-content/uploads/2021/10/Paying-more-for-less-Careers-and-employability-support-for-international-students-at-UK-universities.pdf

Huang, H., & S. Curle (2021) Higher education medium of instruction and career prospects: An exploration of current and graduated Chinese students' perceptions. *Journal of Education and Work*, 34(3): 331–343. https://doi.org/10.1080/13639080.2021.1922617

Jorre de St Jorre, T., & B. Oliver (2018) Want students to engage? Contextualise graduate learning outcomes and assess for employability. *Higher Education Research & Development*, 37(1): 44–57. https://doi.org/10.1080/07294360.2017.1339183

Kinginger, C. (2009). *Language learning and study abroad: A critical reading of research*. Palgrave Macmillan.

Lasagabaster, D., & A. Doiz (2021) *Language use in English-medium instruction at university: International perspectives on teacher practice*. Routledge.

Lea, M.R. (2016) Academic literacies: Looking back in order to look forward. *Critical Studies in Teaching and Learning*, 4(2): 88–101. https://doi.org/10.14426/cristal.v4i2.91

Lea, M., & B. Street (1998) Student writing in higher education: An academic literacies approach. *Studies in Higher Education*, 23(2): 157–172. https://doi.org/10.1080/03075079812331380364

Lillis, T., & M.J. Curry (2010) *Academic writing in a global context. The politics and practices of publishing in English*. Routledge.

Lillis, T., & J. Tuck (2016) Academic Literacies: A critical lens on writing and reading in the academy. In K. Hyland & P. Shaw (Eds.). *The Routledge handbook of English for Academic Purposes* (pp. 30–43). Routledge.

Macalister, J. (2015) Study-abroad programme design and goal fulfilment: 'I'd like to talk like a Kiwi'. In D. Nunan & J.C. Richards (Eds.). *Language learning beyond the classroom* (pp. 235–243). Routledge.

Maloney, E.J., & J. Kim (2020) *Fall scenario #11: Students in residence, learning virtually*. Inside Higher Ed https://www.insidehighered.com/blogs/learning-innovation/fallscenario-11-students-residence-learning-virtually

McArthur, J. (2021) *Rethinking student involvement in assessment*. Centre for Global Higher Education Working paper 58 https://www.researchcghe.org/perch/resources/publications/working-paper-58final.pdf

Nicol, D.J., & D. Macfarlane-Dick (2006) Formative assessment and self-regulated learning: A model and seven principles of good feedback practice. *Studies in Higher Education*, 31(2): 199–218.

QAA & Advance HE (2021) *Education for sustainable development guidance*. QAA & Advance HE https://www.qaa.ac.uk/quality-code/education-for-sustainable-development

Robertson, S., L. Hoare, & A. Harwood (2011) Returnees student-migrants and second chance learners: Case studies of positional and transformative outcomes of Australian international education. *Compare: A Journal of Comparative and International Education*, 41(5): 685–698. 10.1080/03057925.2011.562369

Sakui, K., & N. Cowie (2008) 'To speak English is tedious': Student resistance in Japanese university classrooms. In P. Kalaja, V. Menezes & A. M. F. Barcelos (Eds.). *Narratives of learning and teaching EFL* (pp. 98–110). Palgrave Macmillan.

Su, L.I.W., H. Cheung, & J.R.W. Wu (2021) *Rethinking EMI: Multidisciplinary perspectives from Chinese-speaking regions.* Routledge.

UUK International (2020) *Supporting international graduate employability: Making good on the promise.* Universities UK International https://universitiesuk.ac.uk/policy-and-analysis/reports/Documents/2020/Supporting-international-graduate-employability.pdf

CHAPTER 4

Creating Impact and Quality: The Role of Academic Literacies Practitioners

An Opening Note on Wellbeing

A quote from a study by Blair (2006) I read in preparation for my 2017 volume has stayed with me since: "students catatonic with tiredness and fear" (2006, p. 91). This quote acquired new salience in Spring 2020. Blair's 2006 study was about Art and Design crits, an academic assessment situation that international students find challenging not only because it has potential to stretch their language resource quite substantially but also because the feedback on their artwork leads them to question the work they create, as well as their sense of self as a designer, artist or craftsperson. Similar challenges arise to varying degrees in other academic areas too. Blair (2006) made me more fully aware of the need to acknowledge the role that wellbeing plays in designing and facilitating learning in general and academic literacies provision in particular. In the context of academic literacies provision for postgraduate Product Design students, before the pandemic, I used an article by Desmet and Pohlmeyer (2013) titled "Positive design: An introduction to design for subjective well-being". Discussion started from the positive design framework mentioned in the article—as an illustration of how to identify a core theoretical thread for thesis research and writing, unpack the meaning of the thread and weave it into discussion of qualitative case studies. As we were highlighting chunks of language in each case study that connected theory and the description of practical design examples, discussion turned towards the

L. Blaj-Ward, *Academic Literacies Provision for International Students*, https://doi.org/10.1007/978-3-031-11503-5_4

framework itself. Positive design "enables and/or stimulates human flourishing" through its three facets: design for virtue, design for experiencing a positive affect and design for personal significance (p. 7). My students agreed that this applied not only to tangible products but also to experiences in general, to learning experiences in particular and to the process of building a sustainable career. In the early stages of the pandemic, positive design and wellbeing acquired greater salience.

"Subjective wellbeing" is explicitly mentioned in the Graduate Outcomes survey launched in late 2018 in the UK as the replacement sector-wide measure of student employability. The survey contains four optional questions focused on "subjective wellbeing" (the official label used by GOS). These questions were not included in the preceding version of the survey (DLHE):

- How satisfied are you with your life nowadays?
- To what extent do you feel that the things you do in your life are worthwhile?
- How happy did you feel yesterday?
- Overall, how anxious did you feel yesterday? (https://www.graduateoutcomes.ac.uk/student-q)

These are questions that respondents are asked to engage with 18 months after graduation, on the assumption that academic study increases satisfaction with life and work. Wellbeing, however, should be not only the outcome of graduation but also the precursor of it, permeating the academic study experience overall and being a core part of academic literacies provision.

Wellbeing can be a challenging concept to define. In a SEDA Special publication (Turner and Kalawsky 2020) about wellbeing, a contribution focusing specifically on international students offers the following explanation:

> To develop a learning environment where students from different backgrounds can thrive, means first to provide time and space to unpack assumptions about emotional and cognitive values. Wellbeing lies at the heart of integration, but wellbeing is also a cultural construct. For some, it may be linked to performance or confidence in the public sphere; for others it belongs to more private dimensions. It can be about physical health, a balanced diet or exercise; or equally about a fulfilling social life and feelings of ease, acceptance or belonging. Constructions of wellbeing differ already

among students and practitioners coming from similar backgrounds; they become extremely complex in multicultural contexts made up of different languages, epistemological approaches, faiths and social practices, about the way friendships are formed, leadership is defined and trust is enacted. (Colaiacomo 2020, p. 11)

Colaiacomo (2020) argues in favour of developing context-specific definitions, co-constructed by students and staff, so that "better integration, a higher level of confidence and active participation in university life" (p. 13) can be achieved.

Within the space of academic literacies provision, wellbeing can be enacted in a variety of ways. It can become an explicit part of the provision, through including texts in which wellbeing is the main focus of discussion, to identify ways in which it is approached from different subject lenses or through using wellbeing-related language to model and practise vocabulary development strategies. It can also be an implicit part of the provision, bearing in mind how session facilitators manage the pace of interaction and the sequencing of activities to maintain student energy and interest at an optimum level; by using student names to maximise students' feelings of belonging; and through regularly "taking the pulse" of the learning situation so that appropriate changes can be made.

Wellbeing is not an explicit focus of discussion in existing literature about academic literacies provision. Ongoing needs analysis and appreciation of contextual circumstances are at the core of academic literacies—looking at both the texts and the practices in the target context and at what prior knowledge and experiences international students bring with them into the new learning context to create personally significant learning opportunities. Post-2020, there is a strong case to be made to broaden needs analysis further and look at how whole person development is enabled by an academic literacies curriculum. Contributors to BALEAP's *Narratives of Innovation and Resilience* (Blaj-Ward et al. 2021) have shown how practitioners in the field can respond promptly and creatively in unprecedented circumstances to facilitate learning in ways that account more fully for wellbeing.

A focus on wellbeing in academic literacies provision echoes points made in Motta and Bennett's (2018) "Pedagogies of care, care-full epistemological practice and 'other' caring subjectivities in enabling education", discussed in more detail later in the chapter. Academic literacies practitioners work in settings where there is substantial scope to enact care-full pedagogies. For the purposes of this particular chapter, "practitioners" refers to academic literacies professionals in student-facing roles, delivering teaching or one-to-one provision; academic literacies professionals who design curricula and materials in a specific teaching context and are substantially involved in the trialling and/or use of those materials with students; or academic literacies professionals who have some management, leadership or quality assurance responsibilities but are still engaged directly in student-facing provision. Discussion in the chapter is filtered through these practitioners' perspective on their own practice.

CARE-FULL, IMPACT-FULL PEDAGOGIES FOR HIGH-QUALITY LEARNING

Academic literacies provision is delivered based on a variety of models, and this will inevitably influence the way practitioners can create impact and the way in which they become involved in quality assurance and enhancement. Models vary depending on whether provision is scheduled before or alongside a degree course and whether it has a more general academic focus or is closely aligned to a specific subject area. In some cases, provision places greater emphasis on language; in others, it pays closer attention to broader issues of genre as social practice, scaffolding students' exposure and engagement with a narrower or broader range of text types and assessment formats. Some models afford academic literacies provision credit-bearing status. Provision can be timetabled on a regular, weekly basis or be delivered as a series of one-off workshops. Academic literacies practitioners may or may not work alongside colleagues with an academic subject background or in close collaboration with colleagues focusing on other aspects of students' experience at university (e.g. library specialists, careers consultants or enterprise advisors). What collaboration entails will differ from context to context.

Underpinning discussion of models of provision is a volume on course development in English for Specific Purposes (Basturkmen 2010), which is of substantial value to academic literacies practitioners new to both designing provision and planning to reflect on their growing understanding of effective provision design. Basturkmen acknowledges here, and in a later published chapter (Basturkmen 2015), that English for Academic Purposes (EAP) as a set of practices is built on an increasingly more refined understanding of how "academic" English differs from the language used in other contexts. Rather than create limiting boundaries around "academic", however, Basturkmen (2010) illustrates the course design principles she puts forward with reference to examples from a range of provision types with immediate relevance for the world outside campus walls and traditionally structured university degrees—for example, a course for overseas-trained doctors. Academic literacies, thus, expands to include a variety of forms of learning, which link academic content to the world outside campus walls. These forms of learning are experienced in an academic context and linked in some form or another to an academic qualification. However, the provision aims to develop not only a student's knowledge and ability to use a narrowly defined repertoire of language and communication strategies but also their identity as professionals who can function successfully in different work and study contexts. The knowledge, experience and facilitation style of academic literacies practitioners have a bearing on the way course principles are enacted and the course experienced.

As discussed in Chap. 2, institutions have attempted to establish the impact of academic literacies provision through linking language proficiency and academic outcomes measurable through grades. Quantifiable evidence is perceived by institutional decision makers as a reliable source of information. To build a rich enough picture of provision which can help inform meaningful enhancement decisions, quantifiable evidence needs to be complemented by insights into students' lived experience (the focus of Chap. 3) as well as practitioner perspectives (the focus of this chapter).

One way in which practitioners can gauge the extent to which their care-full practice leads to impactful learning is illustrated in the vignette below:

> *The Learning and Development Centre at Constellations University, a central unit with professional services status, has among its staff a pre-sessional tutor who is in the process of completing a postgraduate certificate in academic practice. As part of his learning, the tutor is required to produce a small piece of research reflecting on the impact of his practice on his students. The tutor was originally planning to combine observation of teaching by a peer with feedback from his students via an online questionnaire. A chance encounter with* Motta and Bennett's *(2018) article prompted a change of plans.*

In their 2018 article "Pedagogies of care, care-full epistemological practice and 'other' caring subjectivities in enabling education", Motta and Bennett do not directly cite academic literacies literature, but their approach resonates fully with the ethos of academic literacies as originally framed by Lea and Street (1998) and Ivanič (1998). Motta and Bennett conducted a piece of research involving interviews and team participatory workshops, framed as a pedagogical "in that researchers and researched are conceptualised as both knowers and learners, and analysis is collaboratively created" (p. 633), taking methodological inspiration from Burke et al. (2016). Insights that were collaboratively co-created centred on care: *care as recognition* that students already possess a range of literacies and knowledge that should be valued and integrated into the learning; *care as dialogic relationality*, based on

> scaffolding learning through reflexively engaging with students through narrative practice of delivery, as opposed to 'classic' lecture style, and using multi-literacies (poetry, newspaper, text, story) and real-world examples with which 'to engage a subject so as to make the concept more real and applicable'. (p. 641)

and *care as affective and embodied praxis*, underpinned by "an awareness of the kinds of rhythms, practices and languages that are conducive to co-creating inclusive and participatory learning spaces and relationships" (p. 642).

The tutor is inspired by Motta and Bennett's article to pilot a series of three participatory workshops offered in addition to the formal academic literacies provision that students already have access to. The workshops draw on multiliteracies and real-world examples as prompts for learning conversations about the kinds of discourse and communication that students find challenging at university. The tutor has a co-facilitator for the workshop. Midpoint, the tutor and co-facilitator stop and introduce the students to an aspect of academic literacies. The midpoint section follows the structure of a formal academic literacies class, with input and space for students to summarise their learning. After the midpoint section, the tutor steps out and the co-facilitator invites students to reflect and feed back on what the tutor could have done differently to create a greater sense of inclusion and belonging. The feedback is summarised (anonymously) for the tutor. The midpoint sections for the three participatory workshops include feedback, reflective writing and critiquing viewpoints, respectively.

The approach the tutor takes aims to counteract what Motta and Bennett (2018) refer to as the careless approach of audit culture and ranking which "reinforces historically deeply gendered and unequal power relations in academe and pushes towards elitist banking approaches in teaching and learning, and instrumental and elitist relationships with society" (p. 635). Motta and Bennett are overtly critical of the emphasis on measurable outcomes and transactional approaches in higher education.

The present volume recognises that there is a place for measurement in higher education and for large-scale surveys if the purpose is collaboratively articulated and shared and if the measurement leads to enhancement being implemented in context-sensitive ways.

Academic literacies provision that builds on Lea and Street's (1998) and Ivanič's (1998) work implicitly endorses the care-full pedagogies that Motta and Bennett value and that lead to impact-full learning. Evaluation of impact in published case studies, however, tends to be framed in more formal and conventional terms, as detailed in the following section.

PRACTITIONERS AS A SOURCE OF IMPACT AND PRACTITIONERS AS EVALUATORS

Different models of practice lend themselves differently to evaluation. Three illustrative examples are discussed below, from Australia, the UK and China, respectively. One example of particular relevance for a discussion of how academic literacies can enhance the quality and outcomes of the student experience is available in Murray and Muller (2019). Starting from the premise that there is "a quite critical lack of alignment between the language focus of university English language gatekeeping tests such as IELTS and TOEFL, and the kind of language students require post-entry in order to navigate the demands of their degree studies" (p. 1349), Murray and Muller introduce a model from the Australian context, built on Lea and Street's (1998) conceptualisation of academic literacies and appreciative of nuances of language learning and use in different disciplines and professional domains. Decentralised provision, they argue, benefits all stakeholders by prompting better collaboration among academic language tutors and academic subject specialists, enhanced outcomes for students, a work environment more conducive to professional development and wellbeing, and greater awareness across the institution of the need to appropriately resource support for students with English as an additional language (EAL). In a semi-devolved model, academic language specialists are based in a central unit but work closely with subject areas within a university. In the decentralised model that Murray and Muller showcase, academic language specialists are based within academic schools, operating "entirely independently of university-wide English language support services and activities" (p. 1353). An office base offering close proximity to subject specialists and regular opportunities to co-teach led to the development of a complex support offer being developed; this included specialist language and genre input, role play of a range of communication scenarios, in-person provision, online content and an online forum as well as bespoke one-to-one support which consisted of "assessing and drawing up study plans for students deemed to be significantly at risk due to weak language skills" (p. 1355). The subject context for the model was Nursing and Midwifery, and student attendance was voluntary.

Following good evaluative practice principles, evaluation of the decentralised model of delivery relied on a combination of data sources: attendance, student evaluations via online feedback and a carefully anonymised survey, peer review of the programme by a nursing lecturer and Chinese speaker of English, a survey administered to nursing staff, student online usage data, and grades. The model was highly appreciated and, with all the caveats associated with the difficulty of disaggregating factors impacting on student outcomes, it was deemed to make a tangible contribution to increasing student performance.

A small number of challenges were identified in relation to implementing the model. Logistical challenges arose with generating a code that the administrative systems could use for scheduling teaching events. Other challenges involved ensuring a consistent understanding, across academic colleagues, of the purpose of integrated academic language provision; greater responsibility for the academic language specialist to build relationships pro-actively; and financial viability across all subject areas, bearing in mind cohort sizes and availability of resource to mitigate against risk associated with insufficient proficiency (relevant in all contexts, but particularly so to Nursing and Midwifery in relation to professional standards and patient safety).

The article is co-authored by an academic researcher and a practitioner involved directly in the delivery of academic literacies provision. The co-authors note that "although [the model] was not implemented as part of a formal empirical study, the School was nonetheless keen to evaluate its performance" (p. 1355). Ethical implications associated with data use are not discussed in the article, and the design and the choice of evaluation tools are accompanied by a brief rationale. The purpose of an academic journal article is to disseminate insights and generate scholarly debate or encourage meaningful application of insights in a broader range of contexts. More detail about the workings and "lived experience" of evaluation lies outside the scope of a journal article but could be disseminated as a complementary piece to facilitate application in different contexts.

A model similar to Murray and Muller's (2019) but delivered in the UK is presented in Calvo et al. (2020). Calvo et al. discuss what they describe as the "Inclusive Collaborative Model", with academic writing integrated into a central module in each year of an undergraduate business degree at a UK university. Their study focuses specifically on the first-year provision and draws on secondary data (student participation in online activities in class and self-access as well as academic essay grades), on 166 responses to a student feedback questionnaire and contributions to a staff focus group (consisting of the module leader, two subject teachers, an academic writing teacher, a graduate teaching assistant and a student learning assistant). The "Inclusive Collaborative Model" was underpinned by Wingate's (2018) approach to integrating academic literacy but went one step beyond by including a postgraduate teaching assistant and student learning assistants as contributors to the module. The writing materials were prepared by the academic writing specialist in collaboration with the module leader and delivered by the subject tutors. The materials were well received, and some participants recommended "developing better guidelines for subject teachers on how to offer the integrated component of academic literacy, as well as advocating for student participation in module design" (p. 11 of 14). The evaluation project that Calvo et al. carried out was set up as a year-long project with institutional ethical approval.

Murray and Muller (2019) and Calvo et al. (2020) make explicit reference to academic literacies in relation to developing and evaluating provision, before the pandemic, and triangulate data sources. Both published studies involve collaboration: between a researcher and an academic literacies practitioner (Murray and Muller), and between an academic literacies tutor, a subject team and student assistants (Calvo et al.). A contrasting example of six English for Academic Purposes practitioners collaborating to evaluate their experience of pivoting online as a result of the pandemic is available in Davies et al. (2020).

Davies et al.'s (2020) evaluation follows a case study format, with six tutors (the article authors) involved in the design and delivery of five EAP courses across four Sino-foreign universities in the early stages of the pandemic-induced global pivot to online education. The themes that structured the reflective exchange of ideas among the tutors (identified as relevant by the lead author) were interaction, learner autonomy, tutor, peer and self-feedback, and leadership and institutional support. The tutors completed retrospective descriptive accounts and collaboratively synthesised insights. The accounts revealed diverse practice, yielding useful insights into how practitioners support each other to develop and implement provision. The spread of the pandemic caught some staff and students away on holiday during the Chinese New Year period; for these tutors and students, the challenge of teaching and studying online was compounded by lack of access to relevant resources and belongings. Another source of difficulty during the pandemic was coordinating course start dates for subject and EAP provision, in the case of embedded support, where official university guidelines were not consistently followed. The authors agree that "it is important to share examples of good practice and to reflect upon the challenges faced at course, programme and institutional level both internally and externally when adopting new modes of educational delivery" (Davies et al. 2020, p. 44). Additionally, they note that insights shared with foreign campuses benefitted implementation of online teaching more broadly across institutions.

The model of academic literacies (or English for Academic Purposes) provision and practitioners' confidence and level of competence with regard to setting up an evaluative project will inevitably vary from context to context. As well as using published studies as examples to design evaluation activities, access to an evaluative framework might be beneficial for practitioners at different stages in their professional journey. An evaluation model developed with regard to a different type of provision (staff learning and development in universities, not academic literacies) but that can be successfully reframed for academic literacies provision is available in Guccione and Hutchinson (2021). Guccione and Hutchinson draw on a pre-existing evaluation model to propose a set of evaluative questions along five different levels. These are detailed below, adapted to refer specifically to academic literacies learning:

Level 0: Inputs and throughputs, which are reported in order to set the context for interpretive commentary.

- The total number of students eligible for academic literacies provision
- The number of unique student engagements with the provision.
- The percentage of students who attend more than one session in cases where provision consists of a series of interconnected sessions logically building on one another.
- The total number of hours of provision offered and attended by at least one student.

- A breakdown of hours of provision by type (e.g. whether cohort-based or individual) and the proportion of induction time to substantive learning time for each type.
- The proportion of students attending who have engaged with the evaluation.
- A breakdown based on "demographic" categories (of immediate relevance would be first language, English language proficiency indicator, main course of study (current or planned)).
- Staff hours including hours of provision delivered, paid or workloaded preparation time, and staff development time (preparation and development time may be more difficult to quantify).

Level 1: Reactions to general communications and broadly administrative matters related to the provision (the "shell" rather than the substance). The framing of student expectations about the provision.

- How clear were the communications to students about scheduling, eligibility and enrolment prior to the start of the provision?
- To what extent did the wording of the aims and anticipated benefits of the provision help set appropriate student expectations?
- How fully did the induction component of the provision support student engagement with the subsequent sessions?
- To what extent did the provision format, location and timing facilitate full engagement?
- To what extent was the provision aligned to students' own learning goals?
- Did the student receive the amount of support they perceived as useful or necessary?
- Were ongoing communications about the provision clear and timely?
- Were students given sufficient opportunities to ask questions about the provision or raise concerns?
- Did students have access to someone they felt could be trusted with confidential and sensitive information about their experience with the provision?

Level 2: Aspects related to learning, which Guccione and Hutchinson (2021) further explain as "expertise, knowledge, insight, skills and attitudinal benefits the participants have gained" (p. 274).

- How well each of the set learning outcomes for the provision were met, based on students' self-evaluation.
- How well the students' self-identified and personalised learning objectives—as set at the start of the provision—were met and to what extent progress has been made, as perceived by students themselves.
- Students' self-evaluated progress against a list of skills used as an audit tool at the start and the end of the provision.
- Students' recounted "moments of sense-making, surprises, key learning points, moments of realisation, revelations, light-bulb moments or insights" (p. 275).
- Students' "feelings about their sense of belonging, motivation, engagement, control over their learning], confidence or happiness" (p. 276).
- Own learning and development reported by staff as a result of delivering the provision—if possible taking a longitudinal view and looking across several iterations of similar or different provision.
- Next steps that students and staff would like to take to continue their development.

Level 3: Behaviour, or how learning was applied.

- Learning that students have been able to apply. How they approach their academic work differently. What has changed for them as a result of engaging with the provision. How others would describe this change.
- Learning that students are intending to apply in a planned opportunity in the near future.

Level 4a: Student outcomes.

- Specific, tangible outputs from engaging with the provision (academic grades would perhaps be an obvious choice here, but tangible outputs could also be completing a portfolio that helps the student secure a placement or internship) and how the provision has supported students to arrive at specific outcomes.
- Evaluations that the student has received from others, with any necessary anonymity and confidentiality preserved.

- Potential forthcoming outcomes: "Exciting developments […] that are on the horizon" (p. 277).

Level 4b: Provider-related outcomes.

- Insights about the student experience that can inform the enhancement of future iterations of provision or that can spark the development of different provision within the same area or in other areas of the university.
- Recurring themes and patterns in the student experience that can help inform decisions in the broader context in which the provision is situated (e.g. student recruitment strategy or course validation procedures).
- Data that can underpin research projects to look at aspects of learning and provision design in more depth.

The five-level framework can be used in full or selectively by practitioners to evaluate their own student-facing practice or to work collaboratively to evaluate a more complex portfolio of provision.

Practitioner Approaches to Academic Literacies Scholarship

In recent years, alongside an increase in published work evaluating academic literacies provision from a variety of angles, attention has focused on the status of academic literacies provision in academia. Discussion has engaged with the precarious nature of a substantial proportion of academic literacies work. It has spotlighted the hierarchical relationship between academic literacies practitioners and the academic communities they serve with the former being perceived as perhaps not fully legitimate members of an establishment built on a foundation of rigorously validated academic subject knowledge. It has argued in favour of reframing the academic literacies practioner role as entailing scholarship of teaching and learning (SoTL, as defined by Boyer 1990, and re-emphasised by Fanghanel et al. 2016) to raise the profile of their work. It has also offered examples of gradual scholarship capacity building, within individuals and teams, ranging from exploring one's own practice within a private, bounded context to sharing this externally, in different formats, for the benefit of wider audiences.

The choice of academic literacies as a label in this volume is partly based on a desire to move away from a restricted understanding of English for Academic Purposes provision as centred on a narrowly defined academic core. The label embraces the complex, multifaceted nature of learning at university. This has a bearing on the nature of the impact created, on the scope of evaluation and on the scholarship that practitioners generate to explore and understand their practice with a view to enhancing its impact on students in a particular context and scaling up its impact on staff development within an institution and across the sector.

At the centre of academic literacies provision is the ambition to support the learning journeys, in English-medium higher education, of students who speak English as an additional language. Given the myriad of forms which English-medium higher education takes (both in countries where English may or may not be the language spoken outside the campus gates or in virtual environments which cut across physical national boundaries), this ambition is most likely to be realised if the variation in university courses is fully acknowledged. Published research into discipline-specific discourse conventions and practices cannot easily keep up with the growth of university courses which take learning outside traditional discipline domains and highlight the value of civic and industry connections. Hence the need for academic literacies professionals to be aware of the existing knowledge base and have the tools and opportunities to gather their own evidence in under-researched areas to ensure that their students are fully supported.

In a 2019 personal viewpoint article published in the *Journal of English for Academic Purposes*, Swales reiterates his lifelong commitment to understanding genre as a complex, multifaceted, lived experience and to fully acknowledging the cognitive, pragmatic, critical and emotional dimensions of learning about and participating in genre events in academia:

> Or consider the case of academic speech, particularly the very common speech event of a conference presentation (often 20 min for the presentation itself, followed by ten minutes for discussion or Q and A). As genre analysts, we will probably want to conceive of both parts as constituting a single speech event. We recognise the presentation consists of a single main speaker, the same participants in the same room at the same time with everybody's attention focused throughout on the main topic (or so the presenter hopes). However, *if we are being EAP practitioners preparing our students for this particular experience, we will (obviously?) opt for two genres because the*

cognitive loads, emotional tensions, and linguistic and rhetorical expectations and affordances of the two parts are very different. In this situation we recognize that the first is basically monologue, while the second is multilogue. Part 1 is prepared (and probably rehearsed); Part 2 is unscripted (and probably in parts unexpected). Finally, the language and paralanguage requirements of the two sections have different exigencies and affordances. In the first, speakers address the whole room; in the second, they serially direct their attention to the various individual questioners and commentators. Finally, in the discussion section, there is likely to be more instances of items like "I think" and "it seems to me" (Wulff et al. 2009). (Swales 2019, p. 76, my emphasis)

There is potential for Swales' point to be expanded further. Swales acknowledges—very helpfully for academic literacies practitioners—that existing genre studies paint an incomplete picture of the nature of discourse in academia and that some have limited "pedagogic import". Further filtering and interpreting needs to be done in order to make the applied linguistic knowledge base more fully relevant to a practitioner context. Swales urges practitioners to "aim for an insider 'emic' approach, even if we cannot always achieve it, because the effort involved in trying to become something of an insider will often produce pedagogical and educational benefits" (Swales 2019, p. 81). A scholarship-oriented understanding of the academic literacies practitioner role is one way to support practitioners to become "something of an insider".

While being fully supportive of Swales' viewpoint with regard to the need to create a body of academic genre knowledge that is more closely relevant to practitioners, I am somewhat troubled by a seeming lack of recognition that EAL users have different levels of language proficiency which will impact on the extent to which they can successfully access genre expectations. I am also troubled by what seems to be an implicit focus on expert, priviledged academic genres rather than looking more holistically at students' experience of learning about genres, the intermediary stages of making sense of expectations associated with a particular academic course. The focus on language, on academic discourse and expertise, and on purpose seems to have been at the expense of people. In an attempt to build academic credibility, EAP practice has favoured "emic" insight into expert academic discourse use over emic insight into EAL experiences or into the range of people and roles that broker successful learning experiences at university.

My volume on *Language Learning and Use in English-Medium Higher Education* (2017a), a journal article which preceded it (2017b) and one which picked up and further developed a thread in the 2017a volume (Blaj-Ward and Matic 2020) gave me the opportunity to explore students' own experiences of making sense of academic discourse and expectations at university in English as an additional language. The interview-based research I conducted, within the standard scholarship and development allocation of an academic contract, was driven by an initial interest in gauging the impact of my own practice of designing and delivering academic literacies provision. At the same time, I wanted to bring to light aspects of students' experience not immediately apparent that I could reflect on, filter through existing literature and use to enrich my own and others' professional knowledge and practice.

Reflection on the insights that my interviewees shared helped me realise that in order to broaden the scope of scholarship and make more visible the complexity of learning interactions that English as an additional language users engage in at university, it was necessary to establish resource and create a platform for scholarship to be disseminated. I secured agreement from BALEAP Executive colleagues to set up BALEAP's Collaborative Practice Funding scheme in 2019, and I coordinated the development work that went into the award process as well as the selection of applicants. The funding scheme had two streams: *Sharing existing good practice to facilitate further professional development* (funding linked to disseminating, at an event, work already carried out) and *Pilot projects* (funding linked to developing new projects). As the award title indicates, in both cases, emphasis was placed on showcasing and catalysing work involving partnership with university staff other than academic colleagues (e.g. learning development, employability, volunteering and student union staff) aimed at "helping students thrive academically and prepare for meaningful, rewarding futures" (BALEAP 2019).

As the two funding streams were a new initiative for BALEAP, the selection criteria were framed as questions to help focus applicants' scholarship ambitions and development and to bring to the fore the importance of ensuring that the scholarship work had clearly articulated links and relevance to students' learning experiences. The criteria for professional development funding prompted applicants to consider the following:

- How did students benefit from the innovative provision offered?
- What did the team designing and delivering the provision learn from this experience that would be of use to other colleagues?
- In what way will the event the applicants have chosen to attend (a) support the professional development of the applicants and (b) help build capacity across the sector for further bespoke provision?

The criteria for pilot project funding encouraged applicants to build a case about the following:

- The extent to which the project is deemed to enhance students' success at university and beyond graduation in the context in which it is delivered
- The extent to which the project paves the way for future collaboration
- Plans to evaluate the impact of the project and ensure longer-term value.

Pilot project applications contained a detailed evaluation plan which aligned with the aim/rationale and workplan, was built into the workplan at various stages (not just a one-off activity at the end), and took account of longer-term impact on all participants involved. They mentioned planned follow-on activity in the applicants' institutional context to indicate longer-term value and plans for sustained impact. They included dissemination plans through a range of media, to ensure impact outside the institution and professional development opportunities for others.

Within the time frame of the Collaborative Practice funding scheme, the stream focusing on sharing existing practice provided funding for two projects to be showcased at annual conferences organised by two significant professional bodies, Advance HE and EATAW respectively (in June and July 2019). Both projects involved initiatives to develop students as academic writers—aligned to academic disciplines but recognising more fully the collaborative work among a variety of higher education professionals to facilitate students' development.

The stream focusing on pilot projects led to five successful applications, on track mid-year in February 2020, then challenged by the unexpected pandemic—these challenges varied depending on the nature of the project, with some pivoting online successfully to achieve intended outcomes and others generating useful learning and reflection about the project. Valuable learning resulted from all experiences in terms of practitioners creating, gauging and sharing impact. One of the two most salient points from that learning was that in order to maximise impact practitioners would benefit from articulating how a particular project fits into the context of their broader work, longitudinally, thinking about their developing expertise and experience facilitating student learning and the way in which student-facing practice and scholarship are intertwined and enrich each other. A project developed by Maria Hussain and colleagues, "Setting up extra-curricular projects with employability colleagues: fostering intercultural student collaboration", connected Maria's classroom practice oriented towards academic learning with her interest in linking this type of learning more seamlessly with lifewide experiences. It enabled her to tap into support from colleagues with an explicit employability remit and to gradually build, on the foundation of her student-facing expertise, a more strategic component providing research-informed advice to support internationalisation initiatives in her institutional context. Impact thus would continue to grow sustainably, crossing the boundary between core curricular literacies and broader learning experiences. Increasing expertise, built on the basis of her experience with smaller-scale scholarship projects, helped amplify her professional voice and broadened the scale on which she could impact.

The second most salient point arising from the Collaborative Practice projects was the importance of ensuring institutional support to enable project success and continued impact. Committed, driven practitioners play a key part in the success of a project. However, to continue to generate impact beyond the time frame of a project, alignment to a strategic priority and links to core activity are needed. Ruth Brooks, a subject specialist working collaboratively with an academic literacies practitioner, led an initiative in her subject area, supported by her university, to develop an employability spine throughout the taught curriculum in an undergraduate degree. Her successful application for Collaborative Practice funding was contextualised within that initiative and her outcomes continue to generate learning value for student cohorts beyond the particular group of students who took part in the project.

The 2019 Collaborative Practice funding scheme was followed by the 2020 Innovative Practice scheme. The 2020 iteration kept the emphasis on rewarding already-developed practice, with a focus on resilient responses to the pandemic and innovations that practitioners had introduced. Eight accounts of innovative, resilient practice in the early stages of the pandemic were shared via an edited collection, and the authors received funding for professional development. The accounts differed in substance and scope, covering postgraduate dissertation writing workshops, in-sessional provision, careers and employability for international students, extracurricular provision focused on wellbeing (an Arts and Crafts channel), student engagement with feedback, pre-sessional tutor induction and organising a staff development conference. What brought the accounts together were the core threads of sustainability and collaboration (the latter salient even in single-authored accounts). As noted in the introduction, to the edited collection, impact was central to the funding scheme:

> The authors of the narratives were asked to consider the depth and relevance of learning that students had gained from the experiences narrated. They were also asked to make recommendations to other institutions that may wish to implement the initiative described. They were advised to accompany the recommendations with discussion of the main learning points for the team that designed and delivered the experience, so that the narrative could lead to further good practice and sustained impact. The narratives offer a range of evidence types and there is recognition that pre-pandemic approaches to feedback collection are in need of reframing so that they capture more fully the value of English for Academic Purposes provision: the personal, academic and professional value of the learning for students, for those who teach and support their learning, and the benefits accrued by the organisations and the communities which welcome international students on their university journeys and beyond. (Blaj-Ward et al. 2021, p. 4)

A CLOSING NOTE

A number of suggestions related to sustainable practice are included at the end of Davies et al.'s (2020) article. These suggestions are raw data from the retrospective accounts written by the article authors exploring their experience as practitioners:

- Strengthen collaboration among instructors to reduce individual burdens (on content creation, etc.)
- Do fewer papers but more papers with multiple drafts so students get in the habit of taking in feedback
- Put limits on the amount of time and effort we put in. Yes, we want to give students good learning experiences even under these difficult conditions, but we also need to pace ourselves and avoid burn-out. (Davies et al. 2020, p. 47)

The suggestions refer specifically to design and implementation of provision, but resonate with evaluation as well, particularly where evaluation is seen as an integral part of a learning and teaching experience.

Collaborative work is part and parcel of academic literacies practitioners' experience. Evaluation of learning and teaching is part of formal quality assurance processes in an institution. As well as serving an assurance purpose, however, evaluation is carried out in order to enhance provision. Enhancement is more likely to be achieved if evaluation is viewed as a form of collaborative scholarship, with institutional quality assurance mechanisms overlapping at least partly with an institution's formal scholarship strategy. Institutional recognition of this relationship would ensure that workload resource is appropriately allocated.

A substantial proportion of academic literacies provision is work of precarious nature, and resource for scholarship may be viewed as secondary to resource for core teaching business. Scholarship contributes to generating impact-full learning, and if collaborative in nature, it has potential to include all practitioners, regardless of employment type. It has potential to be richer and more diverse as a result and to lead to positive outcomes not only for student learning but also for staff career development and progression and for a wide array of communities within and outside campus walls that students and staff participate in. Viewing scholarship only as SoTL—one category in Boyer's (1990) four-part framework—risks offering narrow perspective on learning at university. The integrated view of scholarship that Matthews et al. (2021) propose "for universities, graduates and society to prosper in an unknown future" (pp. 12–13) redresses the balance. Rich and diverse academic literacies provision is linked to scholarship that places equal value on research, on working across disciplinary boundaries and on linking the academy and the wider world.

REFERENCES

BALEAP (2019) *BALEAP collaborative practice funding: Information sheet.* BALEAP https://www.baleap.org/wp-content/uploads/2019/03/info-sheet.pdf

Basturkmen, H. (2010) *Developing courses in English for Specific Purposes.* Palgrave Macmillan.

Basturkmen, H. (Ed.). (2015) *English for academic purposes: Critical concepts in linguistics.* Routledge.

Blair, B. (2006) At the end of a huge crit in the summer, it was 'crap'—I'd worked really hard but all she said was 'fine' and I was gutted. *Art, Design and Communication in Higher Education*, 5(2): 83–95. https://doi.org/10.1386/adch.5.2.83/1

Blaj-Ward, L. (2017a) *Language learning and use in English-medium higher education*. Palgrave Macmillan.

Blaj-Ward, L. (2017b) From language learner to language user in English-medium higher education: Language development brokers outside the language classroom. *Journal of Research in International Education*, 16(1): 55–64. https://doi.org/10.1177/1475240917694109

Blaj-Ward, L., K. Hultgren, R. Arnold, & B. Reichard (2021) *Narratives of innovation and resilience: Supporting student learning experiences in challenging times*. BALEAP https://www.baleap.org/wp-content/uploads/2021/02/BALEAP-Narratives-of-innovation-and-resilience.pdf

Blaj-Ward, L., & J. Matic (2020) Navigating assessed coursework to build and validate professional identities: the experiences of fifteen international students in the UK. *Assessment & Evaluation in Higher Education*, 46(2): 326–337. https://doi.org/10.1080/02602938.2020.1774505

Boyer, E. (1990) *Scholarship reconsidered: Priorities of the professoriate*. Carnegie Foundation for the Advancement of Teaching.

Burke, P. J., G. Crozier, & L. I. Misiaszek (2016) *Changing pedagogical spaces in higher education: Diversity, inequalities and misrecognition*. Routledge.

Calvo, S., L. Celini, A. Morales, J.M.G. Martínez, & P. Núñez-Cacho Utrilla (2020) Academic literacy and student diversity: Evaluating a curriculum-integrated inclusive practice intervention in the United Kingdom. *Sustainability*, 12(3). https://doi.org/10.3390/su12031155

Colaiacomo, S. (2020) Is everything OK? Internationalisation of the curriculum and constructions of wellbeing. In S. Turner & K. Kalawsky (Eds.). *Wellbeing in higher education* (pp. 11–14). SEDA Special 45.

Davies, J.A., L.J. Davies, B. Conlon, J. Emerson, H. Hainsworth, & H.G. McDonough (2020) Responding to COVID-19 in EAP contexts: A comparison of courses at four Sino-foreign universities. *International Journal of TESOL Studies*, 2(2): 32–51. https://doi.org/10.46451/ijts.2020.09.04

Desmet, P.M.A., & A.E. Pohlmeyer (2013) Positive design: An introduction to design for subjective well-being. *International Journal of Design*, 7(3): 5–19. http://www.ijdesign.org/index.php/IJDesign/article/viewFile/1666/587

Fanghanel, J., J. Pritchard, J. Potter, & G. Wisker (2016) *Defining and supporting the Scholarship of Teaching and Learning (SoTL): A sector-wide study*. Advance HE. https://www.advance-he.ac.uk/knowledge-hub/defining-and-supporting-scholarship-teaching-and-learning-sotl-sector-wide-study

Guccione K, & S. Hutchinson (2021) *Coaching and mentoring for academic development*. Emerald Publishing.

Ivanič, R. (1998) *Writing and identity*. John Benjamin's Publishing Company.

Lea, M., & B. Street (1998) Student writing in higher education: An academic literacies approach. *Studies in Higher Education*, 23(2), 157–172. https://doi.org/10.1080/03075079812331380364

Matthews, A., M. McLinden, & C. Greenway (2021) Rising to the pedagogical challenges of the Fourth Industrial Age in the university of the future: An integrated model of scholarship. *Higher Education Pedagogies*, 6(1): 1–21. https://doi.org/10.1080/23752696.2020.1866440

Motta, S.C., & A. Bennett (2018) Pedagogies of care, care-full epistemological practice and 'other' caring subjectivities in enabling education. *Teaching in Higher Education*, 23(5): 631–646. https://doi.org/10.1080/1356251 7.2018.1465911

Murray, N., & A. Muller (2019) Developing academic literacy through a decentralised model of English language provision. *Journal of Further and Higher Education*, 43(10): 1348–1362. https://doi.org/10.108 0/0309877X.2018.1483015

Swales, J.M. (2019) The futures of EAP genre studies: A personal viewpoint. *Journal of English for Academic Purposes*, 38: 75–82. https://doi.org/10.1016/j.jeap.2019.01.003

Turner, S., & K. Kalawsky (Eds.). (2020) *Wellbeing in higher education*. SEDA Special 45.

Wingate, U. (2018) Academic literacy across the curriculum: Towards a collaborative instructional approach. *Language Teaching*, 51(3): 349–364. https://doi.org/10.1017/S0261444816000264

CHAPTER 5

Conclusion

RETHINKING BOUNDARIES IN ACADEMIC LITERACIES PROVISION AND EVALUATION

Unprecedented circumstances have led to carefully thought-out prior plans for learning and development in higher education becoming obsolete and irrelevant. Higher education professionals are learning to walk the road as they build it; to be agile and to appreciate more fully that expertise about learning design on campus lives in many different spaces (Grabill et al. 2022). Academic literacies provision is one space where agility, flexibility and inclusivity exist in abundance. Academic literacies practitioners are ideally positioned to facilitate and participate in conversations about ways to rethink and rebuild higher education—collaboratively—with a view to "helping students thrive academically and prepare for meaningful, rewarding futures" (BALEAP 2019). The way learning is facilitated and experienced has changed. What has stayed the same is the need to ensure quality learning that generates meaningful impact—and this can only be achieved through building a shared understanding, among all stakeholders, of what counts as relevant quality and impact and of the most appropriate road to take to arrive at desired outcomes.

The final vignette in a chapter about quality, relevance and impact from my 2014 volume reads as follows:

L. Blaj-Ward, *Academic Literacies Provision for International Students*, https://doi.org/10.1007/978-3-031-11503-5_5

Claire, the head of an English language teaching centre with staff on teaching and research contracts, is a member of her university's internationalisation committee and is contributing to redrafting the university's internationalisation strategy. Within the remit of this project she has been asked to meet with the heads of the various schools within the institution where she works in order to collect relevant information about each school's approach to enhancing course quality in response to a substantial increase in international student recruitment and about setting partnerships with institutions abroad. This partly overlaps with Claire's doctoral supervision duties. One of Claire's doctoral students is conducting interviews with pro-vice-chancellors and members of other universities' senior management teams about their approach to internationalisation and curriculum review. (Blaj-Ward 2014, pp. 170–171)

The commentary accompanying the vignette notes:

Claire and her PhD student decide to conduct a joint pilot interview with the head of a school at the forefront of internationalisation within the institution where Claire and her student are based. Each of them will conduct half the interview. This will give Claire the opportunity to provide feedback to her student on his interviewing technique (both verbal and body language), while the student will be able to ask Claire questions about aspects he is uncertain about. Having an observer in the room will help with reflecting afterwards on the questions asked, the way in which these could have been rephrased for further clarity, or the way in which follow-up questions could have been asked to gain deeper insight into the topic. (p. 171)

The interview goes well. Claire and her PhD student gather useful insights about various relevant aspects. They are also pleased to note how supportive colleagues in the institution are of international students and how keen to create positive learning experiences for them. Fast-forward to the present day, one could potentially imagine that Claire's PhD student has become an established academic literacies professional at Constellations University, member of a working group that has been tasked with developing his university's global engagement strategy. The former PhD student now leads on the learning-focused thread of the strategy. He has read a recent report (Lewis 2021) about the same topic and has attended a talk in which the report author noted that the most innovative feature of a redrafted global engagement strategy, in her view, was an explicit focus on global social mobility and social justice. He is also still pondering a British Council (2017) document he came across shortly before the pandemic about universities, cities and the future of internationalisation. Among other things, the document states:

> Internationalisation is much more nuanced than international student numbers or foreign direct investment. It is a long-term game where creating an attractive, open, vibrant place to live and work is more important than fluctuations in visitor numbers; where the winners are formerly marginalised communities as well as internationally connected businesses. (p. 31)

The former PhD student's university has been engaging staff, civic leaders and local community members in conversations about how to make the city a welcoming, inclusive place for international students. The next stage of the conversation will be to explore how the curriculum can help bring the university and the city closer together and build capacity for learning and growth in ways that generate direct positive impact for the region in which the university is based as well as in the local, national and global communities to which the university's students and staff belong (Blaj-Ward 2021). This will involve some reframing of existing courses, modules and assessment approaches. Academic literacies practitioners in the university will be required to input both into scaffolding the learning experiences of international students and into evaluating the quality and impact of these experiences. Claire's now former PhD student is also interested in how a relevant virtual experience can be created for international students who study remotely with Constellations University, in different parts of the globe, rather than joining its physical campus. A focus group with alumni is an important part of his approach.

May 2022. Kay recalls a late afternoon in early May 2020, when she was two-thirds of the year into a postgraduate Graphic Design course. She was working on a project about wellbeing—a concept which in her first language had to be paraphrased, because her first language did not have a specific word for wellbeing. Kay also recalls a project she worked on alongside an academic literacies member of staff to develop a "Colouring book for writing: A designer's guide to colouring-in a literature review".

Fast-forward to May 2022, now an alumna, Kay has been invited to attend an online workshop run by Claire's former PhD student, in a time slot deemed convenient for a group of alumni based in different parts of the world (Kay is back in her home country). The workshop aims to explore international student learning experiences during the pandemic; to capture relevant insights into how the learning was linked to the physical place in which the university was located (e.g., through tasks which involved researching the local area or work placement opportunities with local organisations); and to identify how the learning was taken back and applied to generate benefits in the local communities the students rejoined after graduation (or new locations they chose for the next stage in their life).

Digital platforms have made it easier to engage academic literacies stakeholders in evaluation and co-creation of provision. The functionality of online communication platforms allows instant evaluation of activities and suggestions. While transcription of live online interaction does not yet fully accurately reflect what is shared in conversation, it does offer a basis on which to build analysis. A variety of online polling and Q&A tools have been fine-tuned and used extensively, since the start of the pandemic, to gather responses in the moment, as well as over a longer period of time to allow in-depth reflection. Feedback forms administered online allow swifter aggregation of data and make it easier to generate evaluative insights that can lead to impact-full action.

The platform selected for Kay's focus group is one that all participants are familiar with, having used it while studying at Constellations University as well as in other contexts following graduation. This enables discussion to flow smoothly. All participants reflect on the "possible selves" (Papafilippou and Bathmaker 2019) they imagined growing into at the start of their degree course and how these selves "acquire[d] sharper contours as learning journeys unfold[ed]" (Blaj-Ward and Matic 2020, p. 328). They reflect on how academic literacies provision offered a supportive environment in which to develop their ability to communicate with confidence, clarity and care. They share stories about how they made a temporary home in the town where Constellations University is located—about the parks, cafés, museums and libraries, the friendly neighbours and helpful strangers, the local businesses that provided work experience opportunities and greater understanding of how academic knowledge can be made life-relevant. They highlight similarities and differences between the learning they did at university and the learning they are continuing to do. They make suggestions about how additional space can be created in academic curricula and assessment to allow students to make stronger and deeper connections between core academic knowledge in a given subject discipline and complementary perspectives from within and outside academia. Their contributions are carefully recorded and appreciated.

PANDEMIC-RELATED CHALLENGES AND OPPORTUNITIES FOR QUALITY EVALUATION AND ENHANCEMENT

The online pivot in Spring 2020 sparked intensive development of platforms through which to facilitate learning and teaching. At the same time, it has led to higher education institutions rethinking how to integrate these platforms with the systems that collect student records data from registration until graduation and beyond. From a quality assurance point of view, this means that, within appropriate ethical and data protection guidelines, providers can conduct a granular and much more nuanced analysis to inform any steps they take to plan and enhance academic literacies provision. They can establish how to sample students to take part in surveys, based on when the students started their academic journey (before or after the online pivot) and how to use this knowledge to interpret qualitative comments the students make. Additional categories of information were created, with relevance for data interpretation.

The pandemic-related changes that providers had to make in Spring 2020 created unprecedented risk to quality and standards, which was managed as competently as possible by providers. Establishing proof of language proficiency was one of these risks, given the delay in creating a secure protocol to administer language tests on which the vast majority of providers depend to make an informed decision about whether to offer places on courses to international students who speak English as an additional language. Uncertainty about how geographic location would impact on visa status and students' ability to qualify for a degree and have this qualification recognised in countries other than the one where they undertook their studies inevitably impacts on the learning experience these students have overall and the way they engage with academic literacies provision.

Whether academic literacies provision is embedded in core academic modules or facilitates student development more broadly, supporting placements, exchanges or volunteering, wellbeing remains a fundamental focus for academic literacies, as does sustainability. Work placements, international exchanges or volunteering experiences—integrated into a course or contributing via an extracurricular route to the development of students' ability to communicate with confidence, clarity and care—were also affected by the pandemic and in turn impacted on students' sense of belonging in a learning community and on scope for them to engage in meaningful interaction. Belonging and wellbeing are closely interconnected. Institutions with greater levels of digital capacity can create digital communities more swiftly and effectively.

Consideration also needs to be given to institutional capacity to sustain the quality of academic provision over several iterations. At the same time as supporting staff and students to keep up with digital developments and with updates to learning platforms, institutions need to respond sensitively and appropriately to diversity in changing student cohorts, to appreciate shared elements of the student experience and to attend closely to the uniqueness of individual lived experiences.

Collaboration is at the core of academic literacies provision. University curricula that wrap around students to fully support their learning are usually the outcome of collaborative conversations among cross-functional teams of academic and professional services staff in an institution; these conversations include students as equal participants and as experts in how they experience learning. Academic literacies staff input into these conversations. Collaboration, however, can encompass students from various institutions (possibly in different countries) learning together while completing projects that have relevance both for their own development and potentially for institution-external stakeholders who set project briefs. The projects could take place in person, virtually or in hybrid mode. In any of these cases, collecting student satisfaction data about the course overall and about academic literacies provision in particular through a standard questionnaire may be a straightforward activity (although see contributions to Coates et al. 2022, for details on how a student engagement survey delivered in one national higher education system needs to be fine-tuned so that it generates meaningful data from other national systems as well). Quality assurance and enhancement aspects that may be more difficult to achieve are to align or work around differing expectations and processes regarding assessment and the award of credit for learning; negotiating timezone differences to set up meetings in which to gather participant input; making appropriate space in taught curricula for cross-institutional student learning opportunities; or establishing ways in which students can be helped to fully articulate the relevance of these learning opportunities for their career and life aspirations.

High-quality data underpins decisions about how to enhance the quality of higher education learning experiences. Coates et al. (2022) aptly note that "Creating data involves major work; however, making effective use of data to improve education can be even more complex" (p. 4).

Coates et al.'s work centres on large-scale, system-wide surveys of student engagement with learning. The present volume focuses on academic literacies provision specifically; it advocates for an ecologically valid approach to evaluation (Kinginger 2009), in which any major, complex work undertaken is appropriately balanced with the enhancement benefits it is likely to yield. The volume recognises that as there are no one-size-fits-all learning experiences, there are no one-size-fits-all evaluation approaches. Regardless of how evaluation is approached, and the extent to which it is designed to interface with what Motta and Bennett (2018) refer to as care-full pedagogies, there are a number of principles that apply across all contexts. These principles are framed as questions further below, and are intended to be used alongside the evaluative framework put forward in Chap. 4.

Discussion throughout the volume has been premised on a view of academic literacies provision as leading to academic, professional and personal growth. While linguistic research into academic discourse and genre has traditionally interpreted "academic" as referring to core features of communication in discipline-specific communities (see seminal study on theory and concepts in English for Academic Purposes by Bruce 2011), the present volume has interpreted "academic" as inclusive of all learning experiences at university—curricular, co- and extracurricular ones. Lea and Street's (1998) original conceptualisation of academic literacies, with its focus on constructing meaning and identity, continues to be particularly relevant in the current higher education context, where the pandemic has realigned priorities and placed stronger emphasis on the need to work collaboratively across disciplines and functional areas to arrive at relevant solutions to global problems.

Building on this premise, a number of principles stand out. To ensure these principles are applied in an ecologically valid way in evaluation, they should be considered in light of the challenges discussed throughout the section:

- What is the purpose of the provision and how is this purpose interpreted and understood by different participants in and contributors to academic literacies-focused learning experiences?
- What features of academic literacies-focused learning experiences do participants and contributors identify as being of high quality and which are prioritised in terms of fitness for purpose, value for money and transformative potential?

- What academic literacies-focused learning experiences do participants and contributors identify as impactful? Which are linked to intended learning outcomes and which are the outcome of unplanned, serendipitous moments?
- Have all participants and contributors been given equitable space to put forward their views?
- Are all participants and contributors sufficiently familiar with evaluation practices to engage in these confidently, and to share information that can be integrated in meaningful ways and converted into relevant educational enhancements?
- What are the most important audiences for the insights generated through the evaluation activity?
- Which participants and contributors are best placed to implement the changes recommended as a result of the evaluation and what aspects of academic literacies provision can change as a result of the evaluation experience itself?
- Do both the provision and the evaluation contribute to participants' and contributors' wellbeing in appropriate measure?
- Are both the provision and evaluation planned and run in an appropriately sustainable way?

REFERENCES

BALEAP (2019) *BALEAP collaborative practice funding: Information sheet.* BALEAP   https://www.baleap.org/wp-content/uploads/2019/03/info-sheet.pdf

Blaj-Ward, L. (2021) *Impactful teaching and learning in the slow lane.* WonkHE https://wonkhe.com/blogs/impactful-teaching-and-learning-in-the-slow-lane/

Blaj-Ward, L. (2014) *Researching contexts, practices and pedagogies in English for Academic Purposes.* Palgrave Macmillan.

Blaj-Ward, L., & J. Matic (2020) Navigating assessed coursework to build and validate professional identities: the experiences of fifteen international students in the UK. *Assessment & Evaluation in Higher Education*, 46(2): 326–337. https://doi.org/10.1080/02602938.2020.1774505

British Council (2017) *Mutual influence? Universities, cities, and the future of internationalisation.* British Council https://www.britishcouncil.org/sites/default/files/mutual_influence_report-ilovepdf-compressed_2.pdf

Bruce, I. (2011) *Theory and concepts of English for Academic Purposes.* Palgrave.

Coates, H., X. Gao, F. Guo, & J. Shi (Eds.). (2022) *Global student engagement: Policy insights and international research perspectives.* Routledge.

Grabill, J.T., S. Gretter, & E. Skogsberg (2022) *Design for change in higher education.* Johns Hopkins University Press.

Kinginger, C. (2009) *Language learning and study abroad: A critical reading of research.* Palgrave Macmillan.

Lea, M.R., & B.V. Street (1998) Student writing in higher education: An academic literacies approach. *Studies in Higher Education,* 23(2): 157–172. 10.1080/03075079812331380364

Lewis, V. (2021) *UK universities' global engagement strategies: Time for a rethink?* Vicky Lewis Consulting https://www.vickylewisconsulting.co.uk/global-strategies-report.php

Motta, S.C., & A. Bennett (2018) Pedagogies of care, care-full epistemological practice and 'other' caring subjectivities in enabling education. *Teaching in Higher Education,* 23(5): 631–646. https://doi.org/10.1080/1356251 7.2018.1465911

Papafilippou, V., & A.-M. Bathmaker (2019) Transitions from higher education to employment among recent graduates in England: Unequal chances of achieving desired possible selves. In H. Henderson, J. Stevenson & A.-M. Bathmaker (Eds.). *Possible selves and higher education: New interdisciplinary insights* (pp. 111–126). Routledge.

Index[1]

A
Accreditation of provision, 38
Assessment
  criteria, 50, 61
  for learning, 52
  strategy, 23
Authentic assessment, 17, 52, 57

B
BALEAP Collaborative Practice
  Funding (2019), 82
BALEAP course accreditation scheme,
  vi, 13, 16, 36, 37
BALEAP Innovative Practice Funding
  (2020), 84
Belonging, 68, 69, 72, 76, 93

C
Career aspirations, 15, 29, 47
Care-full pedagogies, 69, 71

Civic engagement, 91
Co-creation, 17, 30, 49, 61, 63
Collaboration, 3, 11, 33, 34, 36–38,
  58, 61, 70, 73, 75, 83–85, 94
Communicate with confidence, clarity
  and care, 17, 57, 92, 93
Constructive alignment, 36–38, 45
Context documentation, 37
Course principles, 71
Course representative, 53
Crit, 67

D
Data professionals, 28, 39
Data protection, 34, 93
Data sharing, 34
Data-related capacity, 24, 29,
  34, 39
Decentralised provision, 73
Designated quality roles, 14, 39
Digital citizen, 17, 49

[1] Note: Page numbers followed by 'n' refer to notes.

Distance travelled, v, 26, 34
Document analysis, 13, 36

E
Ecological validity, 95
Embedded academic literacies
    provision, 32
Employability, 15–17, 48, 53,
    54, 56, 57, 63, 68, 82,
    84, 85
English as an additional language
    (EAL), 2, 73
English-medium instruction
    (EMI), 14, 15, 23, 25, 47,
    54, 55, 62
Ethics, 29, 45, 74, 75, 93
Evaluation as social practice,
    13, 16, 23
Evaluation criteria, 10
Evaluation strategy, 10
Evaluation framework (adapted from
    Guccione and Hutchinson
    2020), 76
Evidence base, 4, 33
External examining, 35–38

F
Feedback, 10, 22, 35, 49–53, 55–57,
    60, 62, 67, 71, 72, 74, 75,
    85, 90, 92
Fitness for purpose, 7, 95
Focus group, 75, 91, 92

G
Genre, 50, 70, 74, 80, 81, 95
Graduate Outcomes Survey
    (GOS), 68
Graduate visa (UK), 3, 57

I
Identity, 5, 15, 22, 46, 59, 62, 71, 95
Incidental learning, 9, 52
Inclusive Collaborative Model, 75
In-sessional, 24, 26, 27, 29, 85
Intended learning outcomes, 9, 32,
    35, 45, 96
Interim review, 37
Internationalisation/global
    engagement strategy, 3, 11, 13,
    23, 84, 90

L
Language development brokers,
    15, 17, 47
Language learner and language user, v,
    7, 15, 17, 46, 47, 82
Language Learning and Use in
    English-Medium Higher
    Education, 12, 14, 82
Language proficiency, v, 5, 24, 26, 27,
    30, 32, 45, 46, 62, 71, 81, 93
Language proficiency gain, 16, 31
Learning and teaching strategy, 23
Learning gain, 16, 30–35
Lived experience, 16, 43, 71, 74, 94

M
Mobility, 1, 11, 25, 43, 49, 57, 90
Multiliteracies, 72

N
Narratives of Innovation and
    Resilience (2021), 11, 69
NEAS, 36
Needs analysis, 17, 44, 45, 52,
    55, 62, 69
Negotiated syllabus, 45, 61

O

Observation of teaching, 71
Ownership of quality assurance/
    evaluation, 14, 34, 39, 58

P

Pandemic, 1, 3, 4, 6, 11, 12,
    15–17, 33, 43, 44, 49,
    57, 67, 68, 75, 76, 83, 84,
    90–93, 95
Peer review of courses, 35
Physical mobility, 11, 43
Positive affect, 68
Possible selves, 48, 92
Professional development (of staff),
    14, 15, 26, 33, 36, 37, 50, 52,
    73, 82, 83
Professional standards, 74
Pre-sessional, 24, 26, 27, 29,
    31, 71, 85

Q

QAA, 8, 23, 52
Quality culture, 16, 39
Quality journey (stages in ~), 8, 14
Questionnaire, 13, 22, 62, 71,
    75, 94

R

Recurring themes and patterns, 79
Relatedability, 10
Repertoire of communication
    strategies, 62
*Researching Contexts, Practices and
    Pedagogies in English for Academic
    Purposes*, 12, 17
Retrospective descriptive account, 75
Ripple effect, 23, 62

S

Scholarship, v, 5, 6, 13, 17, 24, 26,
    36, 37, 60, 79–86
Scholarship strategy, 86
Semi-devolved provision, 73
Significance, 31, 68
    statistical *vs.* personal, 31
Standards, v, 4, 8, 13, 14, 31, 36, 37,
    39, 62, 74, 82, 93, 94
Student performance data, 27
Student records, 28, 93
Student satisfaction, 4, 28, 32, 49,
    52, 56, 94
Study abroad, 46
Survey, 4, 22, 68, 73, 74, 93–95
Sustainability, 11–16, 34, 85, 93
Sustainable assessment, 57
Sustainable careers, 52, 57, 68

T

TEQSA, 27, 28
Tracking, 14
Transnational education (TNE),
    3, 23

U

Unplanned, serendipitous learning, 17
Useability, 10

V

Value for money, 7, 95
Virtue, 68

W

Wellbeing, 1, 11–17, 30, 52,
    59, 60, 67–70, 73, 85, 91,
    93, 96